WORKBOOK

English 4 Explorer

Jane Bailey
with Helen Stephenson

NATIONAL GEOGRAPHIC LEARNING | **CENGAGE Learning**

Australia • Brazil • Japan • Korea • Mexico • Singapore • Spain • United Kingdom • United States

English Explorer Workbook 4
Jane Bailey with Helen Stephenson

Publisher: Jason Mann

Commissioning Editor: Alistair Baxter

Assistant Editor: Manuela Barros

Senior Marketing Manager: Ruth McAleavey

Content Project Editor: Denise Power

Production Controller: Tom Relf

National Geographic Liaison: Leila Hishmeh

Cover Designer: Natasa Arsenidou

Text Designer: eMC Design Ltd., UK and PreMediaGlobal

Compositor: PreMediaGlobal

Audio: EFS Television Production Ltd.

Acknowledgments
The publisher would like to thank the following for their invaluable contribution: Karen Spiller and Anna Cowper.

ISBN: 978-1-111-22366-3

National Geographic Learning
Cheriton House
North Way
Andover
Hampshire
SP10 5BE
United Kingdom

Cengage Learning is a leading provider of customized learning solutions with office locations around the globe, including Singapore, the United Kingdom, Australia, Mexico, Brazil and Japan. Locate your local office at:
international.cengage.com/region

Cengage Learning products are represented in Canada by Nelson Education, Ltd.

Visit National Geographic Learning online at **ngl.cengage.com**
Visit our corporate website at **www.cengage.com**

Photo credits
The publishers would like to thank the following sources for permission to reproduce their copyright protected photographs:

Cover photo: Steven Alvarez/National Geographic Image Collection

pp 3 (Shutterstock), 4 (Stephen Shepherd/Alamy), 5 (rolfbodmer/iStockphoto), 6 (Shutterstock), 7 (NASA Goddard Photo and Video), 10a (AP Images/Keystone, Walter Bieri), 10b (Reuters/Howard Burditt), 10c (Howard Burditt/Reuters), 11a (ITV), 11b (Trinity Mirror/Mirrorpix/Alamy), 12 (soloir/iStockphoto), 13 (Photos 12/Alamy), 14 (Shutterstock), 20 (Adrianna Williams/Corbis), 21 (David Page/Alamy), 22 (GlobalP/iStockphoto), 23 (Shutterstock), 24a (kimeveruss/iStockphoto), 24b (Chris Windsor/Getty Images), 24c (sahua/123rf), 30a (MSRPhoto/iStockphoto), 30b (Jbryson/iStockphoto), 31 (Flory/iStockphoto), 33a (RyanJLane/iStockphoto), 33b (Roy Morsch/Corbis), 33c (Ron Chapple/Photodisc/Getty Images), 35 (The Photolibrary Wales/Alamy), 36 (Richard Hewitt Stewart/Getty Image), 40 (Wally McNamee/Corbis), 41a (Ricardo Demurez/Photolibrary), 41b (barsik/Bigstockphoto), 43 (Eriko Sugita/Reuters), 44 (Simon Winnall/Taxi/Getty Images), 45 (jirkaejc/Bigstockphoto), 52 (sculpies/iStockphoto), 54a (guenterguni/iStockphoto), 54b (Paul Thompson Images/Alamy), 55a (PSL images/Alamy), 55d (klenova/iStockphoto), 56 (Shutterstock), 63 (GeorgiosArt/iStockphoto), 64a (Emory Kristof/National Geographic Image Collection), 64b (Kenneth Garrett/National Geographic Image Collection), 68 (James L. Stanfield/National Geographic Image Collection), 74 (Shutterstock), 75 (Marka/Alamy), 76 (Photos 12/Alamy), 77a (Don Cravens/Time Life Pictures/Getty Images), 77b (World History Archive/Alamy), 79 (Shutterstock), 80 (Arco Christian/Photolibrary), 85 (igorr1/iStockphoto), 86a (djeecee/iStockphoto), 86b (travelstock44/Alamy), 86c (ugurhan/iStockphoto), 87 (moodboard/Alamy), 91a (Shutterstock), 91b (Arek Tkacz), 92a (Shutterstock), 92b (Shutterstock), 92c (Shutterstock), 92d (Shutterstock), 96a (Shutterstock), 96b (Reuters/Corbis), 96c (Peter Bennett/Ambient Images/Photolibrary), 97a (Richard Nowitz/National Geographic Image Collection), 97b (FrankvandenBergh/iStockphoto), 97c (Stephen St. John/National Geographic Image Collection), 98a (Raul Touzon/National Geographic Image Collection), 98b (AchimHB/iStockphoto), 99a (J. Baylor Roberts/National Geographic Image Collection), 99b (Shutterstock), 100a (l.weeber/Fotolia), 100b (Douglas Miller/Hulton Archive/Getty Images), 100c (Shutterstock), 101a (AmandaLewis/iStockphoto), 101b (Shutterstock), 101c (Robert Harding World Imagery/Getty Images), 102a (Sisse Brimberg/National Geographic Image Collection), 102b (James L. Stanfield/National Geographic Image Collection), 103a (H.M. Herget/National Geographic Image Collection), 103b (Mark Thiessen/National Geographic Image Collection), 104a (Kazuyoshi Nomachi/Corbis), 104b (North Wind Picture Archives/Alamy), 104c (James L. Stanfield/National Geographic Image Collection), 105 (Michal Knitl/Shutterstock.com), 106a (Bentley Archive/Popperfoto/Getty Images), 106b (London Daily Mail/National Geographic Image Collection), 106c (Mary Evans Picture Library/Alamy), 107a (Colin Pacitti/Alamy), 107b (Michael Nichols/National Geographic Image Collection), 108a (Shutterstock), 108b (Jib_meyer/iStockphoto), 108c (Shutterstock), 109 (Lynn Johnson/National Geographic Image Collection), 110a (W.E. Garrett/National Geographic Image Collection), 110b (mgfoto/iStockphoto), 110c (The Trustees of the British Museum), 111 (Superstock/Photolibrary)

Illustrations by Celia Hart (pp 30, 34, 53, 56, 62, 88); Janos Jantner (Beehive Illustration) (pp 3, 32, 42, 57, 78); Dave Russell (pp 65, 104, 108); Norbert Sipos (Beehive Illustration) (p 18); Eric Smith (pp 19, 41, 75, 79)

Printed in Singapore by Seng Lee Press
Print Number: 06   Print Year: 2016

Revision

Grammar: present simple and present continuous

1 Complete the text with the present simple or present continuous form of the verbs in brackets.

Hi. I'm Adrian. I ¹...................... (play) rugby for my school team and this is a picture of me and my friends. I'm in the middle and I ²...................... (wear) the team shirt. My friends ³...................... (watch) me play about twice a month, when we ⁴...................... (compete) at home. My best friend, Jay, ⁵...................... (enjoy) playing sport too, but he's not competitive. He ⁶...................... (prefer) going to the gym and he ⁷...................... (go) running every day. That's my girlfriend, Hannah on my left. She's really kind and friendly. We ⁸...................... (smile) in this picture. That's because the team ⁹...................... (win) the league and there ¹⁰...................... (be) only one match left to play.

2 Write questions about the text in Exercise 1.

1 Where / Adrian / stand / in the picture?
....

2 How often / Adrian's friends / watch / him play?
....

3 Jay / like / sport?
....

4 What / Jay / do / every day?
....

5 What / Hannah / be / like/ ?
....

6 Why / everyone / look / happy/ ?
....

Vocabulary: *do* or *make*

3 Complete the sentences with the present passive or active form of *do* or *make*.

1 Sam is lazy. He never .... any housework.

2 A lot of mistakes .... in exams because students get nervous.

3 Children .... friends easily.

4 Who .... that terrible noise?

5 The washing-up .... by machine.

6 What .... pizzas .... from?

Grammar: permission and obligation

4 Complete the text with the words in the box.

| allowed | can | can't |
| has to | let | mustn't |

Jade's parents are originally from Iran. They're quite strict about a lot of things. For example, Jade isn't ¹...................... to stay out late, even at weekends. When she goes out, she ²...................... tell them where she's going and she ³...................... wear make-up or high heeled shoes.
At home, they're more easy-going. They ⁴...................... her have lots of friends round and they ⁵...................... stay as long as they like. However, they ⁶...................... play loud music or bring boys round.

Vocabulary: phrasal verbs

5 Complete the dialogues with the correct form of the phrasal verbs in the box.

| break up | fall out | get on with | look after |
| not go out with | take after |

1 A: What's your girlfriend's name?
  B: Actually, I .... anyone at the moment.

2 A: Ben wants to .... with Claire.
  B: Why? They're perfect for each other.

3 A: The twins argue and fight a lot, don't they?
  B: Yes, they do. They .... always ....

4 A: Who do you ....?
  B: Well, I look like my mum, but I'm quiet and serious, like my dad.

5 A: Can I borrow your new bike, please?
  B: OK. But you must .... it!

6 A: Why does Sam hate school on Mondays?
  B: Because he has PE and he doesn't .... the teacher.

Vocabulary: Asking for information

6 *R.1* Jade wants to find out about the swimming club disco. She rings the swimming club coach. Listen and complete the notes.

Swimming club disco

Day: ¹...................... Time: ²......................

Place: ³......................

Price: ⁴...................... including ⁵......................

Who's going? The ⁶...................... team

Revision

Grammar: the past

1 **Complete the dialogue with the past simple or past continuous form of the verbs in brackets.**

Gran: ¹...................... (you / enjoy) the school trip yesterday?

Emma: Yes. It was great! We ²...................... (travel) to Oxford on the bus, then we went to the Bodleian library. After that, we ³...................... (go) on a tour of the colleges. Oh! And Robert Smith fell into the river!

Gran: What ⁴...................... (you / do) on the river?

Emma: We ⁵...................... (try) to punt! Robert ⁶...................... (rock) the boat from side to side when he ⁷...................... (lose) his balance and fell in. It was really funny!

Gran: Poor Robert! So, ⁸...................... (you / learn) anything useful on this trip?

Emma: Of course. While we ⁹...................... (look) round the buildings, we ¹⁰...................... (find out) a lot about Oxford's history and architecture.

2 **Complete the text with the words in the box. There is one extra word.**

| lots | many | most of | much | was | wasn't | were (×2) |

I went to high school in the 1980s. It was an ugly, tall, grey building. There ¹...................... about eight classrooms on every floor. There was also a science laboratory and a dining hall, but there ²...................... an IT room – not like today! In fact, I don't think there ³...................... any computers at all. There ⁴...................... a large canteen on the ground floor. Not ⁵...................... students stayed for school dinners because the food was awful! ⁶...................... us used to take our own sandwiches. There were ⁷...................... of good teachers at the school. They made us work hard in class, but we didn't usually have ⁸...................... homework.

Grammar: relative pronouns and relative adverbs

3 **Complete the sentences with** *when, where, which, who, whose* **or** *that*.

1 Damien Hirst, ... became famous in the 1990s, produces strange works of art.

2 Hirst often uses dead animals, ... many people find shocking.

3 Van Gogh spent a lot of time in France, ... he eventually died.

4 He didn't earn any money for his paintings .... he was alive.

5 Banksy is a street artist .... work is often funny and controversial.

6 Anthony Gormley's *Angel of the North* is a sculpture .... took three years to make.

Grammar: the passive

4 **Rewrite the sentences using the active or passive form.**

1 I was given a guitar for my birthday by my aunt. My ....

2 Hirst sold his diamond skull for £50 million. Hirst's diamond skull ....

3 They didn't choose me to be in the school play. I ....

4 A New York record producer discovered Missy Elliot. ....

5 Freddie Mercury's parents sent him to boarding school. ....

6 Bob Marley released his first songs in Jamaica. ....

Vocabulary: performers and artists

5 **Complete the sentences with the correct form of the words in the box.**

| art | classic | exhibit | perform | success | talent |

1 My cousin is very .... She loves painting and drawing.

2 Mozart was a .... musician and composer. He began playing the piano when he was only four years old.

3 I love listening to .... music, especially Bach and Beethoven.

4 Leona Lewis has sold lots of records and is now a very .... singer.

5 I thought last night's .... of *Othello* was brilliant!

6 Did you see the art .... at Central Gallery?

Revision

Grammar: the present perfect

1 Write sentences. Use the present perfect and add *for* or *since*.

1 I / not see / the dentist / two years.

....

2 They / live / in this neighbourhood / 20 years.

....

3 You / not take / your medicine / this morning.

....

4 I / not be / ill / last year.

....

5 Ravi / not win / a competition / 2009.

....

6 Max / have / a bad cough / two weeks.

....

2 Complete the text with the present perfect or past simple form of the verbs in brackets.

I ¹..................... (put on) a lot of weight last month, so I ²..................... (decide) to go on a diet. It's not a strict diet – just healthy eating, really. I ³..................... (not eat) any junk food for four weeks and I ⁴..................... (lose) three kilos since I started! I ⁵..................... (join) a gym last week. Unfortunately, I ⁶..................... (be) busy this week, so I ⁷..................... (only / go) to the gym twice.

3 Rewrite the sentences and the question in the present perfect. Use the words in brackets.

1 I took a painkiller a minute ago. (just)
I've ....

2 Mary had her vaccinations the other day. (already)
Mary has ....

3 Paul has still got the flu. (not recover / yet)
Paul ....

4 Lily went to the leisure centre about an hour ago. (already)

....

5 There was a car accident here a few minutes ago. (just)

....

6 Are you still waiting to see the doctor? (not see / yet)

....

Grammar: reported speech

4 Complete the reported statements and questions with the verbs in the box. Add any other words.

ask	order	remind	tell	warn

1 'Put down that gun now!'
The policeman .... the robber to put down his gun.

2 'Don't forget to make an appointment at the dentist.
My mum .... to make an appointment at the dentist'.

3 'Go and sit down in the waiting room.'
The receptionist .... sit down in the waiting room.

4 'Can you lie down on the couch, please?'
The doctor .... to lie down on the couch.

5 'Don't eat anything before the operation – it's dangerous!'
The nurse .... anything before the operation.

5 Complete the dialogue. Match the missing sentences (1–7) with the options (a–g).

Jack: ¹...

Abby: I've hurt my ankle and I can't play hockey!

Jack: ²...

Abby: Yes it is! The school championships are next week and I've been training really hard! It's just not fair!

Jack: ³...

Abby: Yes, I have. He said ... He said ...

Jack: ⁴...

Abby: He said I'd torn a muscle badly and he told me not to do any sport for six weeks.

Jack: Look.⁵...

Abby: I suppose so. I'm just so disappointed!

Jack: ⁶...

Abby: Good idea. I haven't eaten anything since lunchtime.

Jack: ⁷...

a That's not so bad.

b Come on. Cheer up! Let's go and get a snack.

c What's wrong?

d Me neither.

e It's not the end of the world. You can compete in the finals next year.

f Go on! What did he say?

g Calm down. Have you been to see the doctor?

Revision

Grammar: the future

1 Complete the predictions with *may, might, might not, will* or *won't*.

1 In the future, all cities .... be enormous. (I'm sure)

2 I think that the buildings .... be taller and more high-tech. (I'm sure)

3 Cars .... exist any more. (it's possible)

4 People .... travel around by jetpack or sky-train. (it's possible)

5 Everyone .... do their shopping online. (I'm sure)

6 As a result of online shopping, there .... be any shops. (it's possible)

7 There .... be any wildlife left in the parks because of the pollution. (it's possible)

8 There .... be more crime. I think society will get better. (I'm sure)

2 Complete the dialogue. Use *going to* for plans and intentions and *might* for predictions.

Ellen: What are your plans for the summer?

Josh: I'm not sure. I ¹..................... (go) trekking in India.

Ellen: Wow! Isn't that a bit dangerous?

Josh: I don't think so. I ²..................... (find out) more about it first, though. So, what about you? What ³..................... (you / do) this summer?

Ellen: Well, first of all, I ⁴..................... (visit) family back in Scotland. We ⁵..................... (spend) about three weeks there. We haven't decided what to do next. We ⁶..................... (catch) a ferry to Norway or we ⁷..................... (hire) a car and drive down to the Mediterranean.

Josh: It all sounds really exciting! I've never been to Scandinavia. I ⁸..................... (go) there instead of India.

3 Circle the correct option.

The council have made new plans for the city centre. They ¹ *'re going to / will* provide more facilities for young people. First of all, they ² *'re going to / will* build a new youth centre, but they haven't decided exactly where to build it yet. They ³ *might / 're going to* build it next to the station, but I don't think anyone ⁴ *will / 's going to* go there. It's too far from the centre. Secondly, the council ⁵ *are going to / might* re-open the ice rink in December if the work on the youth centre finishes on time. However, I think that this is unlikely and that the ice rink probably ⁶ *isn't going to / won't* be ready before next year.

Grammar: indirect questions

4 Put the words in the correct order to make indirect questions.

1 where / guidebook / tell / I / can / a / buy / you / me / can /?

....

2 near / do / hostel / you / there's / is / if / here / know / a /?

....

3 somebody / how / could / works / machine / ticket / explain / the /?

....

4 do / know / the / to / open / visitors / when / is / cathedral / you /?

....

5 train / our / does / know / anybody / what / leaves / time /?

....

6 costs, / much / how / this / could /souvenir / me / you / mug / tell / please /?

....

5 Put the dialogue in the correct order.

.... **a** Oh hi, Mr Prim. It's Sandra. Could you give him a message, please?

.... **b** Can you tell him we're going to book the tickets to Prague tomorrow?

.... **c** With pleasure. What's the message?

.... **d** Hello. Can I speak to Tim, please?

.... **e** You're welcome.

.... **f** Yes, of course. I'll tell him as soon as he gets in.

.... **g** Sorry, he isn't at home at the moment. This is his dad speaking.

.... **h** Thanks very much, Mr Prim.

Revision

Grammar: conditionals

1 Complete the text with the first conditional form of the verbs in brackets.

Earth is home to the most amazing creatures and natural wonders imaginable. But what ¹...................... (happen) to the planet if we ²...................... (not look after) it? The truth is that if we ³...................... (not be) careful, we ⁴...................... (turn) our beautiful world into a desert environment, where many plants and animals ⁵...................... (not survive). If we ⁶...................... (continue) to cut down the forests, we ⁷...................... (destroy) the natural habitat of many endangered species. Tigers and pandas ⁸...................... (become) extinct. Another danger is pollution. If factories ⁹...................... (carry on) polluting the seas and rivers, this ¹⁰...................... (kill) smaller fish and other sea creatures. As a result, there ¹¹...................... (not be) enough food for whales and sharks.

2 Write second conditional sentences and questions. Use the verbs in the box.

> be (×2) be able to eat invent not pour recycle
> save slow down survive turn off not use

1 If everybody .... their rubbish, our environment .... cleaner.
2 If scientists .... an alternative to plastic, we .... recycle more waste.
3 We .... a lot of water if people .... the tap more often.
4 More sea creatures .... if factories .... industrial waste into the rivers.
5 .... global warming .... if we .... cars anymore?
6 If we .... less meat, there .... more land available to grow food for everyone.

Grammar: quantifiers

3 Circle the correct option.

1 Volcanic eruptions are *much / very* dangerous.
2 Max thinks lightning is *a bit / quite* exciting.
3 I think hurricanes are *much / quite* more destructive than tornadoes.
4 It's true that solar energy is *a lot / very* environmentally friendly.
5 Being a volunteer is *a bit / really* good fun.
6 Volunteer work can sometimes be *a bit / lot* tiring.

Vocabulary: prepositions

4 Complete the text with the prepositions in the box.

> about (×3)   to   out   over   up

Are you worried ¹...................... the environment? Do you want to learn more ²...................... problems in your area?

If so, then come and join us!

Green Schemes is an environmental group which helps people to find ³...................... about how to improve their local area. At our meetings, you will be able to talk ⁴...................... expert ecologists and lawyers. We have also written a letter to the council to complain ⁵...................... the new buildings which are taking ⁶...................... our countryside.
If you are interested, just turn ⁷...................... at our next meeting! We meet every Wednesday in the community centre at 7 p.m.

Vocabulary: advising and suggesting

5 Vicky and Mark are helping to plant trees. Complete the dialogue with the options (a–g).

Mark: ¹...................... me to help you plant that tree?

Vicky: Yes, please. It's quite big and heavy.

Vicky: Excuse me, I need a shower but there's no hot water. ²......................

Leader: ³...................... complain to the campsite manager.

Manager: Good evening. ⁴...................... do for you?

Vicky: The hot water has run out in the shower block.

Manager: Sorry, there won't be any more until tomorrow morning. ⁵......................, I'd get up early and be first in the queue.

Mark: There are loads of mosquitoes in my tent!

Vicky: ⁶...................... use insect repellent and a mosquito net?

Mark: ⁷...................... where I can get a mosquito net?

Manager: Yes, of course. You'll find one in the cupboard at the end of the corridor.

> **a** If I were you   **e** Can you tell me
> **b** Would you like   **f** What can I
> **c** You should   **g** What should I do?
> **d** Why don't you

1A Fans

Vocabulary: mass media

1 Complete the crossword.

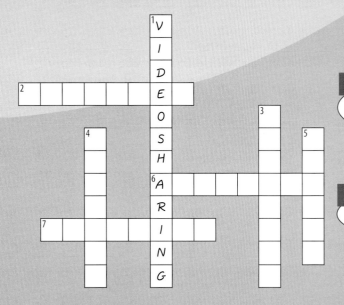

Across

2 You read them in newspapers and magazines.

6 You are part of this when you watch a play or concert.

7 The title of a newspaper story.

Down

1 Letting other people see your video files.

3 Satellite TV has many of these.

4 A video or audio file that you watch or listen to online or download to your iPod.

5 A person who watches TV.

2 Circle the correct option.

1 There are *lots of / not much* soap operas on TV.

2 I watch TV *more than / most of* five times a week.

3 The producer cancelled the new soap opera because it doesn't have *many / much* viewers.

4 How *often / many* hours a week do you watch TV?

5 I *always / never* listen to the radio in the mornings. I love the breakfast show.

6 *How much / How many* times a year do you go to the cinema?

7 *Which / How* is your favourite TV programme?

3 Complete the statements with the words in the box. Then match the statements (1–6) with the people (a–d).

front page   listeners   programme   readers   ~~station~~   website

1 Tune in to Big FM, the local *station* with the best music and the latest news.

2 This .... is live from the O2 stadium. I'm Mike Hadley and I'm talking to you from outside the stadium.

3 One of our .... has phoned in to request a song for his girlfriend.

4 Our regular .... often send in letters and photos, and we publish the best ones.

5 It's an important article, so I think it will be on tomorrow's ....

6 Go to our .... to find out more about the stories in this month's issue.

a newspaper journalist ☐
b magazine editor ☐ ☐
c radio DJ ☐ ☐
d TV reporter ☐

Grammar: present simple and present continuous

4 Write sentences. Use the present simple or present continuous form of the verb.

We / love / X Factor.
We love X Factor.

1 Maggie / never / go / to the theatre.
....

2 Jason / always / take / the bus to school.
....

3 Shhh! The students / do / an exam.
....

4 Which part / you / play / in the musical?
....

5 Penny / write / an email / at the moment.
....

6 Max / know / lots of / famous people.
....

5 Write the questions.

How often do you watch TV? (watch / TV)
I usually watch TV every night.

1 ....? (like /
Leona Lewis) Yes, I do. I think she's fantastic!

2 ....? (do)
I'm listening to music on my MP3.

3 ....?
(concert / start) At seven o'clock.

4 ....? (laugh)
Because this programme is really funny!

5 ....? (read)
My geography book. I've got an exam tomorrow.

6 ....?
(have / singing lessons) Once a week.

Grammar: present perfect

**6 Match the sentences with the functions. Write
a, b or c next to each sentence.**

a an action in the past with a result in the present
b a past action in a time period which includes
the present
c life experiences

Have you ever joined a fan club? [c]

1 Lady Gaga has released a new album. ☐
2 I've never taken part in a talent competition. ☐
3 Look! Thousands of fans have joined the
queue for tickets. ☐
4 It's the first time I've been to a concert. ☐
5 The *Star Trek* fans have dressed up as their
favourite character. ☐
6 Oh no! It's started raining on the sound
equipment! ☐

**7 Complete the statements and questions. Use the
present perfect form of the verbs in the box.**

be	~~borrow~~	fall	go	sign	sing	vote

Sally *has borrowed* my camera again without
asking!

1 A: Where's Will?
B: I think he .... to bed.

2 .... you ever .... to the opera?

3 Melanie .... never .... for
anyone on *X Factor*.

4 Look at all the famous people who ....
my autograph book!

5 One of the contestants .... off the
stage. We're taking her to hospital.

6 It's the first time Mike .... in a
competition. He's nervous!

Grammar: present simple, present continuous and present perfect

**8 Complete the interview with the correct form
of the verb in brackets.**

Presenter: What's your name and where *have you
travelled* (you / travel) from today?

Maggie: I'm Maggie and [1] ....
(I / drive) here from Scotland.

Presenter: Is this the first time [2] ....
(you / audition) on *X Factor*?

Maggie: Yes, it is. But [3] .... (I / be) in
other talent competitions before.

Presenter: Really? [4] .... (you / ever / win)
any of them?

Maggie: Yes, actually. [5] .... (I / usually /
come) first in the competitions that
[6] .... (I / enter).

Presenter: Great! So [7] .... (you / feel)
confident about today?

Maggie: Actually, [8] .... (I / be)
a bit nervous. This is the biggest talent
competition in Britain. Also, millions of people
[9] .... (watch) *X Factor* on TV
every week and [10] .... (I / not
perform) in front of such a big audience before.

Presenter: I'm sure you'll be fine. So, Maggie, what
[11] .... (you / sing) for the
judges today?

Maggie: [12] .... (I / choose) my
favourite song by Leona Lewis – Bleeding Love.

Working with words: verb + preposition *at* and *to*

**9 Write sentences in the present simple
or present continuous. Add the correct
prepositions.**

The band / talk / their fans / outside.
The band are talking to their fans outside.

1 Why / that boy / stare / me ?
....

2 Look! The audience / throw / flowers / the
dancers.
....

3 The photographer / point / his camera / you /
but / not take / any pictures / at the moment.
....

4 They / write / notes / each other / in class /
every day.
....

5 Those girls over there / look / a magazine /
and / laugh / some funny cartoons.
....

Reading

1 **What do you know about the famous people in the photos? Tick (✓) the statements you think are true.**

1 They have each donated more than $5 million to charity. ☐

2 They all work for UNICEF. ☐

3 They have all received awards for their charity work. ☐

2 **Now read the text and check your answers to Exercise 1.**

3 **Read the text again. Are the sentences true or false?**

	T	F
1 Nowadays, most famous people give money to charity.	☐	☐
2 Brad Pitt has recently donated $5 million dollars to a well-known charity.	☐	☐
3 Politicians are not interested in celebrities and their charities.	☐	☐
4 Bono has met with world leaders several times to discuss his charity work.	☐	☐
5 Some people think that celebrities only do charity work because it is good publicity.	☐	☐
6 The 'Nobel Peace Laureate' awards are special awards for celebrities who do a lot of work for charity.	☐	☐
7 Bono has won the Nobel Peace Prize more than once.	☐	☐

Charitable celebrities?

These days the majority of celebrities are involved in charity work. Most actors, singers, musicians, politicians and sports stars support different charities by donating money. Some celebrities give more than others and some have donated huge sums of money. One of these stars is actor Brad Pitt, who has donated around $5 million to different charities over the years.

But it's not just about money. Many celebrities also give lots of time and energy to supporting big charities and promoting their campaigns all over the world. Celebrities can help charities in other ways too, for example in the media attention they can attract. They might also have direct contact with politicians and other powerful people and can make them listen. Bono, for example, has had meetings with several presidents, including the former US President, George Bush, and the Pope to talk about his charity work. UNICEF, the United Nations

Children's Fund, invites one or two celebrities every year to become Goodwill Ambassadors for their new campaigns. Recent UNICEF Ambassadors include David Beckham and Shakira as well as actors Orlando Bloom and Selina Gomez.

Some people say that charity work has become just another way for celebrities to promote themselves. However, some stars have worked so hard to promote peace and defend human rights that they have received a special award from the Nobel committee. The Nobel Peace Laureates awards recognise people in the entertainment industry for their hard work and commitment to different charities. Bono, Annie Lennox and George Clooney are recent winners – and Bono has been recommended for the Nobel Peace Prize three times. Yes, charity work is good publicity for celebrities, but it's also good publicity for the charities and the people who need their help.

Vocabulary: TV shows

4 Complete the sentences with the words in the box.

> act audition episode judge rehearsal ~~repeat~~ winner

There's nothing good on TV tonight. It's either sport or a *repeat* of *Celebrity Come Dancing*.

1 I really like this new TV series. When's the next .... on?

2 That boy can .... really well. I think I've found the next Leonardo di Caprio!

3 Michelle has gone to a(n) .... for a part in a soap opera. I hope she gets it!

4 The .... of last year's talent show is now a TV presenter.

5 My favourite .... on *X Factor* is Simon Cowell.

6 The final .... before the play opens is on Wednesday night.

Working with words: noun + noun

5 Complete the sentences with compound nouns. Use a word from box A and a word from box B for each gap. Use plurals where necessary.

> **A** crowd head film film mind museum news slide sports summer
>
> **B** clothes control line location official paper report review scene show

1 The teacher is showing us a s..................... .... of photos of her trip.

2 The m..................... .... was angry when tourists started taking pictures.

3 Some people believe that you can move objects using only m..................... ....

4 The f..................... .... was the Sahara desert, so the actors got very hot.

5 There are lots of dramatic c..................... .... in the film with hundreds of people in them.

6 My dad loves reading the n..................... .... on Sundays.

7 He looks quickly at the h..................... ...., but he doesn't read the news articles properly.

8 He loves football and tennis and spends hours reading the s..................... ....

9 My mum loves cinema, so she enjoys reading the f..................... .... most.

10 I must buy some new s..................... .... to wear on holiday.

Grammar: *yet, still, already* and *just*

6 Complete the sentences and questions with *yet, still, already* or *just*. Put the verbs into the correct tense.

Although Andrew is three years old, *he still can't talk*. (he / can / not talk).

1 Wait for me! I .... and I'll be downstairs in two minutes. (get / my coat)

2 Josh is only nine months old but he ....! (can / walk)

3 Although it only came out a week ago, the new girl group .... of their new album! (sell / one million copies)

4 I'm sorry, I .... here, so I don't know all the students' names yet. (start / work)

5 It's getting very late. Why ....? (you / be / here)

6 I have to write an article about Madonna before tomorrow, but I ....! (not start / it)

Listening

7 🔊 *1.1* **Listen to a podcast from a website for English language learners. What is the podcast about?**

a this year's film and TV awards

b soap operas around the world

c popular British TV soap operas

8 Listen again and answer the questions. Write the name(s) of the programmes, or write *both*.

Which programme(s)

are popular in other parts of the world? *both*

1 can you watch if you live in Sweden? ....

2 has been on TV the longest? ....

3 has more real-life drama? ....

4 has recently won a lot of awards? ....

5 attracts the most viewers? ....

6 has a younger audience? ....

Exchanging opinions

Useful expressions

1 Put the words in the correct order to make useful expressions.

I / he's / think / talented / really

I think he's really talented.

1 unfriendly / she / bit / seems / me / a / to

....

2 opinion, / they're / best / girl / in / group / my / the

....

3 you / know / mean / I / what

....

4 say / you / that / do / why / ?

....

5 because / he's / funny / really / that's

....

6 so / don't / think / I

....

7 think / you / so / do / ?

....

2 Read the dialogue. Match the statements and questions (a–f) with the gaps (1–5).

Zoe: This article looks interesting. It's called *Hollywood Favourites – Who Gets Your Vote?* You have to vote for your favourite actors and actresses. The first category is coolest male actor.

Kim: That's easy. I think the coolest actor is Robert Pattinson.

Zoe: Really? ....*f*.......

Kim: ¹ .... of course! And he's a great actor too.

Zoe: I agree. He's brilliant in the *Twilight* films! What about the best male singer?

Kim: That's easy too! It's Joe Jonas from The Jonas Brothers.

Zoe: ² .... In my opinion Nick is the best.

Kim: ³ ....

Zoe: Yes, I do. ⁴ .... You know that he's got a solo career now as well, don't you?

Kim: Yes, I know. He's got a great voice, but I think Joe is better-looking.

Zoe: ⁵ .... I love his hair! So, what about the coolest female actress?

Kim: I'm not sure. Maybe Miley Cyrus.

a Do you think so?
b I don't think so.
c He's a really talented singer, in my opinion.
d Because he's handsome,
e That's true.
f Why do you say that?

3 Read the statements and questions. Choose the best response (a, b or c).

Why do you think Britney Spears is annoying?
(a) Because she behaves badly.
b Do you think so?
c I don't think so.

1 I think there are too many repeats on TV.
a Because they're boring.
b I think so.
c That's true.

2 Why do you think he's going to lose the contest?
a I think he's popular.
b Because he's not talented.
c I don't think so.

3 Victoria Beckham is only famous because she's married to David.
a Why do you say that?
b Yes, she does.
c Because she's a pop singer.

4 There are lots of great programmes on TV these days.
a That's because I like stories about vampires.
b I think they're fantastic!
c That's true. But they're all about celebrities!

5 The Harry Potter books seem a bit childish to me.
a Because they're about magic.
b I think so.
c I know what you mean.

Pronunciation: past participles ending in -ght and -ghed

4 Think about the pronunciation of *bought* and *coughed*. Write the past participles of the verbs in the box in the correct column in the table.

| bring | ~~buy~~ | catch | ~~cough~~ | fight | laugh | teach | think |

bought	coughed
....	....
....	....
....	....
....	....
....	....

5 ⊙ *1.2* **Listen and check.**

Writing: a review

6 Read the film review. Match the information (1–5) with the paragraphs (a–c). You can use the letters more than once.

1 what the film is about ....
2 good points ....
3 the main actors ....
4 who will like the film ....
5 bad points ....

7 Complete the review with the sentences.

a Taylor Lautner is the best actor, in my opinion.
b On the other hand, the special effects are not very good.
c In conclusion, the film is interesting and most teenagers will enjoy it.
d On the one hand, the film is very entertaining.
e The vampires look very realistic.

8 Complete the sentences with *because* or *because of*.

1 Bella is unhappy .... she misses her boyfriend.
2 Edward has split up with Bella .... his family.
3 Edward's family are dangerous .... they are vampires.
4 .... the bad special effects technology, the wolves just made people laugh.
5 Boys will like the film .... it has lots of action.
6 The film is disappointing .... its weak ending.

9 Make notes about a film you have seen recently. Organise your writing into three or four paragraphs. Then write your film review in your notebook.

A review of *New Moon*

a *New Moon* is the second film in the *Twilight* series. It has recently come out on DVD. The film stars Kristen Stewart as Bella and Robert Pattinson as Edward. Bella is very sad because Edward, her boyfriend, has broken up with her. But this is because he is a vampire and he wants to protect Bella from his friends and family. Bella spends a lot of time with her friend Jacob, who is a native Indian. He belongs to a gang that can turn themselves into wolves.

b ¹ .... There is a lot of action and romance. I also think that the acting is quite good. ² .... He plays Jacob and is good in the romantic scenes as well as in the fight scenes. The vampire scenes are also very good.
³ .... This is because of the excellent make-up.
⁴ .... The audience laughed at the computer generated wolves when they first appeared on the screen. They did not seem real and were so bad that they were funny.

c ⁵ .... There is lots of romance for the girls and plenty of action for the boys. However, the film doesn't have a strong story and the ending is disappointing.

Details and format
Title: ....
DVD / cinema? ....
Genre: ....
Main actors: ....
Basic plot: ....

Good points
....
....
....
....
....

Bad points
....
....
....
....
....

Conclusion
....
....
....

Reading

1 Put the sentences in the correct order.

.... **a** Millions of people watched her audition on YouTube.

.... **b** After *Britain's Got Talent* finished, Susan released her first album.

.... **c** In April 2009, Susan Boyle auditioned for the TV programme *Britain's Got Talent*.

.... **d** However, she didn't need to win – she was already an international star.

.... **e** It sold millions of copies all over the world.

.... **f** Susan only came second in the competition.

2 Put the sentences in the correct order.

Hi Kim,

.... **a** Have you seen it yet?

.... **b** If you haven't, do you want to come with us?

.... **c** Jason and I are going to the cinema on Saturday.

.... **d** We can meet you outside the cinema at 6.30 p.m.

.... **e** We're going to see *Twilight*.

Zoe

Listening

3 **1.3** You will hear four statements twice. Match each statement with the correct response (a–c).

1 ....

a What do you think of them?

b I didn't enjoy it.

c Do you think so?

2 ....

a I don't think so.

b Yes, I have. I saw it last weekend.

c It seems boring to me.

3 ....

a Because there are lots of repeats.

b What did you watch?

c Why do you say that?

4 ....

a That's true.

b I don't like it.

c Do you think so?

Word list Starter Unit and Unit 1

actually (adv)	....	mad about (adj phr)	....
announce (v)	....	major (adj)	....
apparently (adv)	....	majority (n)	....
award (n)	....	make an appointment (phr)	....
battle (n)	....	male (adj)	....
calm down (phr v)	....	on the one hand (phr)	....
celebrity (n)	....	on the other hand (phr)	....
clumsy (adj)	....	performance (n)	....
competition (n)	....	podcast (n)	....
conclusion (n)	....	ponytail (n)	....
contestant (n)	....	publicity (n)	....
convention (n)	....	queue (n & v)	....
(a) couple of (n)	....	rehearsal (n)	....
deadline (n)	....	reveal (v)	....
disappointed (adj)	....	rumour (n)	....
disaster (n)	....	soap opera (n)	....
donate (v)	....	split up (phr v)	....
dull (v)	....	stage (n)	....
emphasise (v)	....	stare at (v)	....
endangered (adj)	....	stunning (adj)	....
episode (n)	....	support (v)	....
female (adj)	....	surround (v)	....
front page (n)	....	survey (n)	....
generate (v)	....	survival kit (n)	....
gossip (n)	....	video-sharing (n)	....
hairstyle (n)	....	viewer (n)	....
headline (n)	....	vote (vote)	....
imaginable (adj)	....	wildlife (n)	....
industry (n)	....	wonder (n)	....
investigate (v)	....		
jetpack (n)	....		
judge (n)	....		
lens *pl* lenses (n)	....		
loads of (n pl)	....		

present simple, continuous and perfect

present simple and present continuous

We use the **present simple** to talk about:

- a regular activity, a habit, an activity often repeated.
  I watch TV almost every night.
- a permanent state.
  Karen works in a TV studio.
- facts, general truths, laws of nature.
  Water boils at 100°C.

We use the **present continuous** to talk about:

- an activity in progress – that is, happening now, at the time when we are talking.
  The stars are arriving at the awards ceremony now.
- a temporary situation, around the time when we are talking.
  He's waiting to hear if he's got the job he applied for.

verbs without a continuous form

Some verbs are called 'stative' or 'state' verbs because they describe a state, feeling or thought rather than an action. We don't normally use the present continuous with these verbs. They include:

believe, hate, know, like, love, need, prefer, seem, sound, think, understand, want

I hate reality TV shows. (Not: *I am hating ...*)

1 Complete the questions with the present simple or present continuous form of the verbs in brackets.

Do you watch (you / watch) this programme every week?

1 How often .... (they / go) out with their friends?

2 Why .... (Joe / want) to get Wayne Hill's autograph?

3 .... (you / believe) the latest story about Paris Hilton?

4 Who .... (you / send) that text message to?

5 Which reality show .... (your parents / like) most?

6 .... (I / play) my music too loud? I'm sorry – I'll turn it down.

present perfect

We use the **present perfect** to talk about:

- an action that happened during a period of time that started in the past and goes up to the present. Exactly when the action happened is not mentioned.
  I've watched 'The X Factor' a few times.

- a state that began in the past, but continues up to the present.
  He's been their lead singer since the band started.
- an action that was completed a very short time ago. (This is almost always used with *just*.)
  They've just introduced the contestants.
- an action that happened sometime in the recent past, but has a result in the present.
  He isn't on the show tonight because he's broken his leg.

> We can use **ever** and **never** with the present perfect to refer to experiences. We use *ever* in questions and *never* in negative sentences. *Ever* and *never* always go before the main verb.
> *Have you ever met a rock star?*
> *I've never been on TV.*
>
> We can also use **It's the first/second time ...** with the present perfect to talk about experiences.
> *It's the first time I've (ever) watched a show like this.*
>
> We can also use **for** and **since** with the present perfect. We use *for* to talk about duration and *since* to talk about when a state or situation started.
> *She has been a teacher for six years.*
> *She has been a teacher since 2005.*

present perfect and past simple

We use the **present perfect** to talk about something happening in the past, as long as the action or time period has some connection with the present. To talk about a completed action at a finished time in the past, we use the **past simple**.

He isn't on the show tonight because he's broken his leg.

He isn't on the show tonight. He broke his leg last week.

2 Write sentences. Use the present simple, present continuous or present perfect form of the verbs.

It / be / the first time / I / be / in a TV audience.
It's the first time I've been in a TV audience.

1 I / think / this / be / the best reality show / I / ever / see.

....

2 The audience / really / enjoy / tonight's concert / and / it / just / start.

....

3 Paul / collect / autographs. He / collect / more than a hundred.

....

4 I / wait / for Emma. I / hope / she / not forget / about our date!

....

5 Sasha / sing / really well, so / she / join / the school choir.

....

yet, still, already and just

yet

We use *yet* with the **present perfect** or the **present simple** in questions and negative sentences. *Yet* always goes at the end of the sentence or clause.

– **Have** you **seen** her new hairstyle **yet**?
– No, I **haven't seen** it **yet**.

– **Is** dinner ready **yet**?
– No, it **isn't** ready **yet**.

still

We use *still* with the **present perfect** in negative sentences. *Still* with the present perfect always goes immediately before *haven't/hasn't*.
I **still haven't decided** what to wear tomorrow.

We use *still* with the **present simple** or **present continuous** in questions and affirmative sentences.

Still with the present simple goes before the main verb, but after the verb *be*.
I'm not a child any more, but I **still like** watching cartoons.

Still with the present continuous goes after the auxiliary *be*.
I'**m still trying** to decide what to wear tomorrow.

already

We use *already* with the **present perfect** or the **present simple** in affirmative sentences.

Already with the present perfect usually goes between *have/has* and the main verb.
She's very young, but she **has already become** a famous TV star.

Already with the present simple usually goes before the main verb, but after the verb *be*.
I **already know** how this story ends.

just

We usually use *just* with the **present perfect** in affirmative sentences. *Just* goes between *have/has* and the main verb.
A new series **has just started** on Channel 4.

3 Complete the sentences and questions with the correct form of the verbs in brackets.

Have you finished (you / finish) your homework yet?

1 Andy .... (still / try) to learn the words of the new song.

2 .... (you / just / switch on) the TV? You .... (already / miss) the best part!

3 Bob .... (already / speak) three languages and now he .... (learn) Spanish.

4 .... (you / still / want) to watch the show tonight?

5 Jackie .... (not buy) tickets for the concert yet.

because and because of

Because and *because of* are used to introduce the reason for the action, state, opinion, etc mentioned in the main part of the sentence.

Because is followed by a clause – that is, subject + full verb.
I love listening to her **because she's got** such a good voice.

Because of is followed by a noun or noun phrase.
This is a depressing film **because of all the violence**.

4 Match the actions/states/opinions (1–5) with the reasons (a–e).

1 I'm studying tonight.	c	**a** all the names and dates
2 We can't have a picnic.	☐	**b** we agree about everything
3 History's a boring subject.	☐	**c** I've got a test tomorrow
4 Anika's my best friend.	☐	**d** it's raining
5 There aren't any buses today.	☐	**e** a public transport strike

5 Write one sentence for each pair in Exercise 4. Use *because* or *because of*.

1 *I'm studying tonight because I've got a test tomorrow.*

2 ....

3 ....

4 ....

5 ....

2A Animal minds

Vocabulary: the mind

1 Complete the quiz questions with the words in the box.

> creative   forget   imagine   memory
> remember   ~~sad~~   think   understand

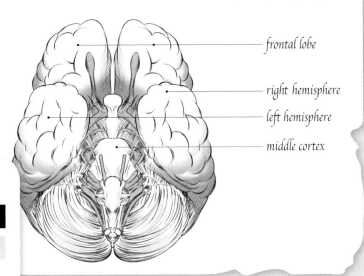

frontal lobe

right hemisphere

left hemisphere

middle cortex

Quiz: Your Mind

Section A: How much do you know?

1 Which part of the brain do you use when you are doing maths?

  a the left side
  b the right side
  c the front

2 Why do people in northern countries often feel *sad* ?

  a Because they don't like the cold.
  b Because they [1] .... about their problems too much.
  c Because they don't get enough sunshine.

3 How many words can babies [2] .... when they are born?

  a They can recognise short sentences.
  b They recognise a few words.
  c none

4 Which group of people have the largest corpus callosa (the area that connects the left and right sides of the brain)?

  a right-handed people
  b left-handed people
  c [3] .... people

Section B: How good is your [4] ....?

5 How often do you [5] .... to do your homework?

  a Never. I always do my homework.
  b Only when I've got a lot of other things to do.
  c Often. I'm hopeless!

6 [6] .... you are seven years old again and back at primary school. How many of your classmates' names can you [7] ....?

  a almost all of them
  b more than half of them
  c less than half of them!

2 Answer the quiz questions. Then read the solutions below.

Solution
Section A: 1a 2c 3c 4b
Section B: If you answered 'a' to both questions, you have an excellent short-term and long-term memory. If you answered 'b' to either of the questions, you have a good memory. If you answered 'c', you need to improve your memory!

3 Circle the correct option.

Most dogs can *feel /* (*understand*) instructions.

1 The students have behaved badly today and the teacher is very *angry / afraid*.

2 Don't *remember / forget* to buy some ink for the printer.

3 Experts believe that elephants have a good *memory / remember*.

4 My grandmother's got a lot of *imagination / memory*. She tells wonderful stories.

5 Children love doing *creative / intelligent* activities like painting and drawing.

6 I can't *understand / imagine* what it's like to live in the desert.

Working with words: abstract nouns

4 Complete the sentences with the words in the box.

> ambition   behaviour   danger   ~~education~~   fear
> friendship   happiness   success   truth

Harry had a good *education*. He went to the best schools and to a top university.

1 My .... is to be a brain surgeon.

2 Do newspaper journalists always write the ....?

3 At my school, we lose marks for bad ....

4 Arachnophobia is the .... of spiders.

5 .... does not come from having lots of money.

6 Animals usually sense .... before humans do.

7 We met when we were children and our .... has lasted twenty years.

8 The pool party was a great ....

Grammar: present perfect continuous

5 Write sentences. Use the present perfect continuous form of the verbs.

Jenny / practise / the violin.

Jenny has been practising the violin.

1 They / play / rugby.

....

....

2 The scientist / look at / something under a microscope.

....

....

3 The children / make / a cake.

....

....

4 The boys / fight / again.

....

....

5 He / not work / very hard.

....

....

6 I / not sleep / well / this week.

....

....

6 Complete the questions. Use the present perfect simple or continuous form of the verbs in brackets.

1 How long *have you been doing (you / do)* your homework?

2 How long .... (Tina / collect) shells?

3 How long .... (Greg / be) in your band?

4 How long .... (Sarah / know) John?

5 How long .... (you / wait)?

6 How long .... (Dad / make) those shelves?

7 Now match the questions (1–6) with the answers (a–f).

a All day! And he still hasn't finished them. ☐

b She's been doing it for about six years. ☐

c For over half an hour! ☐

d I think they've been friends since they were at primary school. ☐

e He's been with us for about two months. ☐

f Since I got home from school, about two hours ago. I'm really fed up with it! ☐

8 Complete the sentences with *for* or *since*.

I've been playing chess *since* I was four years old.

1 The cat's disappeared. We haven't seen it .... yesterday.

2 Sanjay's been upstairs on the computer .... hours!

3 The dogs haven't been out for a walk .... this morning.

4 Michelle has been going out with Tim .... three months.

5 James hasn't had a haircut .... ages. He looks awful!

6 The children haven't had anything to drink .... they arrived.

9 Complete the dialogue with the correct form of the verbs in brackets.

Aisha: *I've been trying* (try) to solve this maths problem for half an hour, but ¹............................. (not work out) the answer yet.

Charlie: Why ²............................. (you / not ask) the teacher to help you?

Aisha: I ³............................. (hold) my hand up for ages. ⁴............................. (you / not notice)?

Charlie: No, sorry. I ⁵............................. (look) down at my textbook most of the time.

Teacher: Aisha, Charlie. ⁶............................. (you / already finish) all the exercises?

Aisha: No. I ⁷............................. (do) the last question. I ⁸............................. (wait) for you to come over and help, sir.

Teacher: Sorry, Aisha. I ⁹............................. (be) very busy. OK. Let's see your book. Hm, I think the main problem is that you ¹⁰............................. (not understand) the basic formula ...

2B Mind control

Listening

1 🔵 **2.1 You are going to hear a scientist talking about the way technology affects the human brain. Listen and tick (✓) the things he mentions.**

- [ ] extroverts
- [ ] intelligence
- [ ] mind control
- [ ] hand-eye
- [ ] pathways in
- [ ] fast reactions
- [ ] memory
- [ ] social skills
- [ ] co-ordination
- [ ] the brain

2 Listen again. Are the sentences true or false?

		T	F
1	It is too early to be certain that technology affects the way the brain works.	☐	☐
2	When we read books, we process more information more quickly than when we use the Internet.	☐	☐
3	Using technology a lot creates new pathways in the brain.	☐	☐
4	Using technology trains our minds to behave less like computers.	☐	☐
5	People who play video games a lot often develop better hand-eye co-ordination.	☐	☐
6	Dr Jarvis is particularly interested in the effect of technology on how doctors work.	☐	☐
7	Young people who spend a lot of time using technology could lose certain social skills.	☐	☐
8	Understanding how people are feeling by reading the expression on their faces isn't an important social skill.	☐	☐

Grammar: relative clauses

3 Write definitions with the words.

Kanzi / a chimpanzee / play the piano.

Kanzi is a chimpanzee that plays the piano.

1 Football / a sport / people / play / all over the world.

....

2 Sheep / animals / can recognise faces.

....

3 A comedian / a person / good at / tell jokes.

....

4 The weekend / a time / people / relax.

....

5 A surgery / a place / doctors work.

....

6 Damien Hirst / an artist / work / be very expensive.

....

4 Join the sentences to make one sentence. Make the second sentence into a relative clause using the relative pronoun in brackets. Put commas in the correct place.

Michael has been on Derren Brown's show. He lives in our street. (who)

Michael, who lives in our street, has been on Derren Brown's show.

1 Chess has been around for centuries. It's my favourite board game. (which)

....

2 Mrs Clark has just had a new baby. She works at the bank. (who)

....

3 The Christmas holidays are great fun. My cousins come to stay. (when)

....

4 Bono has done a lot of work for charity. His real name is Paul Hewson. (whose)

....

5 Luigi's restaurant is famous for its pasta dishes. My mum works there. (where)

....

Reading

5 Read the text and match the paragraphs (1–3) with the headings (a–d). There is one extra heading.

a A clever pair   **c** Animal artists

b Tricking the trainers   **d** Great escapes

Animal tricksters

Have you ever played a trick on someone? If so, then you know that you need to think and prepare carefully for your trick to work. You have to guess how the person will act. Then you have to find a way to trick them. In other words, you need to be quite intelligent.

1 ....

Some animals have proved their intelligence by playing tricks on humans. A dolphin named Kelly knows how to trick her trainers to get more food. They taught her to keep her pool clean by collecting the rubbish that fell into it. When she gave it to a keeper, she got a tasty piece of fish as a reward. Now, when paper drops into her pool, she takes it to the bottom of the pool where she hides it. When the trainers come, she swims down and tears off a small piece of paper. She gives it to the trainer, who gives her some fish in exchange. Kelly also knows that big pieces of paper get the same reward as small pieces, so she only tears off small pieces to make the paper last longer!

2 ....

Other animals have used their brains to think of escape plans. One female elephant used her intelligence to escape from the animal park where she lived. She used her trunk to take off the bolts on a locked gate. Then she opened the gate and let all the elephants out. Apes are skilled escape artists. They have been escaping from their cages since the day zoos were first invented. They are very creative and have used every trick in the book to get out of their enclosures. They have stolen keys from their keepers, built ladders and picked locks. One orang-utan even used sticks to damage the wires to a security fence. She then escaped without getting an electric shock.

3 ....

Pigs are also clever creatures. Take the story of 'The Tamworth Two'. These two British pigs showed amazing skill and intelligence when they decided to escape the slaughterhouse. They dug a hole under a fence, swam across a freezing river and were on the run for more than a week. In the end, they were captured but they did escape the knife. The two pigs, which became famous all over the world, now live in comfort at an animal sanctuary. Their adventures have been the subject of a BBC film and a TV drama as well as many stories and articles.

6 Read the text again and answer the questions.

Which animal(s) mentioned in the text:

1 tricked some humans by using their knowledge of how they react?

2 used logic to understand how electricity works?

3 escaped from certain death?

4 regularly escape from captivity?

5 helped other animals to escape?

6 became international stars?

7 Choose the correct answer (a, b or c).

1 It's necessary to be quite intelligent if you want to:

   a train dolphins.

   b play a trick on someone.

   c work with animals.

2 Kelly's trainers rewarded her with extra fish if she:

   a collected bits of rubbish.

   b found big pieces of paper.

   c did tricks underwater.

3 How did the female elephant use her trunk to escape?

   a She took the lock off a gate.

   b She knocked down a gate.

   c She unlocked a gate with a key.

4 Apes that live in zoos:

   a don't often escape.

   b have used books to play tricks.

   c have often shown a lot of intelligence by escaping.

5 The Tamworth Two:

   a have become animal actors.

   b now have a comfortable home.

   c have recently escaped from an animal sanctuary.

Useful expressions

1 Put the words in the correct order to make checking sentences. Some have question tags.

she / cat's / isn't / lovely, / my / ?

My cat's lovely, isn't she?

1 exam / the / isn't / Friday / next / ?

....

2 having / a / aren't / party, / they're / they / ?

....

3 pet, / a / doesn't / he / he / have / does / ?

....

4 to / we / the / going / aren't / tomorrow / presentation / ?

....

5 at / left / you / home / your / book / have / ?

....

6 told / before, / you / I haven't / I / have / this / ?

....

2 Match the first part of the question (1–8) with the correct question tags (a–h).

1 It's a lovely day,   **a** is it?
2 We've already seen this film,   **b** aren't you?
3 Paul's on holiday this week,   **c** does she?
4 It isn't time to leave yet,   **d** isn't it?
5 She doesn't like presentations, **e** are we?
6 You're coming with us,   **f** are you?
7 We're not inviting Jim and Sally, **g** isn't he?
8 You aren't interested in this,   **h** haven't we?

3 Choose the correct option (a, b or c) to complete the dialogue.

A: It's Billy's birthday next week, [1]...........?

B: Yes. He's having a party on Saturday, [2]...........?

A: Yes. [3].......... got your invitation yet?

B: No. Perhaps I'm not invited.

A: Of course, you're invited! Billy sent the invitations online. You've checked your email recently, [4]...........?

B: No! I'll go and look. What can we get Billy for his birthday?

A: He can paint really well, [5]...........? We can get him some really good oil paints.

B: They're a bit expensive, [6]...........?

A: You're right. It would cost too much.

B: I know! [7].......... recently started doing judo?

A: Yes, he has. Why don't we get him a bag for his sports kit?

B: Great idea!

1 a isn't he   **b** isn't it   **c** is he
2 a isn't he   **b** is he   **c** has he
3 a Do you   **b** You have   **c** Haven't you
4 a have you   **b** do you   **c** haven't you
5 a can't he   **b** does he   **c** doesn't he
6 a are they   **b** do they   **c** aren't they
7 a Doesn't he **b** Hasn't he   **c** Has he

4 Sean and Jana are entering their dog, Lady Gaga, in a dog show. Complete the dialogue with the words in the box.

| can   does   doesn't   don't   ~~haven't~~   isn't |

Jana: Come on, Sean, we need to get Lady Gaga ready. You've brought the dog brush with you, *haven't* you?

Sean: Yes, of course. It's in the bag with the other things.

Jana: Now, which colour ribbon looks best? I think the pink one is prettiest, [1].................... you?

Sean: I'm not sure. I think she needs a brighter colour. Red would look good with her white fur.

Jana: Hmm. Poor old Lady. She doesn't look very happy, [2].................... she?

Sean: I know. Actually, she looks a bit stupid with the ribbon in, [3].................... she?

Jana: Yes, she does. I don't think we should put one in at all.

Sean: But she needs something. She can't see with all that hair in her eyes, [4].................... she?

Jana: That's true.

Sean: So ... red or pink?

Jana: I don't mind. You choose. But hurry up! It's nearly time for the show to start, [5].................... it?

Sean: You're right. We've only got two minutes left! OK. Let's use the red one.

Pronunciation: question tag intonation

5 **🔊 2.2 Listen to the questions. Which question tag does not have falling intonation? Repeat the questions.**

1 Elephants have very long memories, haven't they?
2 You haven't already seen this film, have you?
3 Kim's been playing the violin for six years, hasn't she?
4 The iPad is like an iBook, isn't it?
5 Your cousin lives in Bangkok, doesn't he?
6 We haven't got to read this book as well, have we?

Writing: a description of people

6 **Read Katie's description of herself. Choose the best adjectives to describe her personality.**

a introvert and shy
b extrovert and sporty
c intelligent and artistic

7 **Complete Katie's profile. Circle the correct options.**

Hi, I'm Katie. I'm really sociable and love meeting new people. I ask lots of questions, *which* / *who* makes people think I'm nosey. This isn't true at all – I'm just ¹ *very* / *a bit* interested in everyone!

I'm ² *a lot* / *very* good at sport, especially football. In the town ³ *that* / *where* I live, there isn't a girls' team, so I have to play in the local boys' team. My sister, ⁴ *whose* / *which* favourite hobbies are ballet and drama, thinks I'm mad! But it's great fun and I don't mind being the only girl. The coach has also asked me to be the team captain this year. My best friend, Alison, ⁵ *whose* / *who's* known me for years, says this is because I'm ⁶ *really* / *a lot* bossy.

Apart from sport, I like listening to music and reading. My favourite time of the day is ⁷ *when* / *where* I come home from school. I go up to my room, ⁸ *which* / *that* is calm and peaceful, put on a CD and relax on my bed. I'm not a messy person, so it's usually clean and tidy and I stay there until my mum calls me for my tea.

One other thing: I'm ⁹ *quite* / *very* superstitious. I don't walk under ladders, but I don't mind the number thirteen and I love black cats!

8 **Complete the sentences with a relative pronoun.**

People *who* don't know Katie think that she's nosey.

1 Her hobbies, ... are football and music, are not the same as her sister's.
2 The pitch .... Katie plays football is in her home town.
3 Katie's room, ... is always tidy, is her favourite place.
4 Katie's best friend, ... name is Alison, doesn't play football.
5 In the afternoons, ... she gets home from school, Katie listens to music.

9 **Make notes about your personality. Choose adjectives and write down ideas for each adjective. Use the example to help you.**

Name: Jem

Personality	Example	Extra information
extrovert	I'm sociable and go out with my friends a lot.	I like talking to people, finding out about them.
funny	good at telling jokes – people laugh at them	My friends, who go to the same school as me, say I'm funny.
very messy	There are lots of dirty clothes in my bedroom.	I don't like tidying my room.
quite clever	get good marks	'A's in my exams last month
a bit moody	I feel annoyed when my mum tells me to tidy my room.	I quite often fight with my little brother.

10 **Complete Jem's personal description. Include the example information from Exercise 9.**

Hi. I'm Jem. I'm an extrovert. I like talking to people and ¹ .... about them. I also like going out. At the weekends, I don't like staying at home. I ² .... with my friends – I'm very ³ .... My friends, who go to the same school as me, say that I'm ⁴ .... because I'm good at telling jokes. People always laugh at them. I think I'm quite clever because I usually get ⁵ .... at school. In my exams, which I did last month, I got all 'A's. My bad points are that I'm very messy. My bedroom, where I do my homework, has ⁶ .... all over the floor. Sometimes I'm a bit moody too. I don't like tidying my room and I feel ⁷ .... when my mum tells me to do it!

11 **Now write your own personal description. Use your notes from Exercise 9 and use relative pronouns where possible.**

Reading

1 Read part of a text about cats and match the correct heading (a–c) with the paragraphs (1–2).

   a Superstitions in the past

   b Black cats in Europe

   c Different beliefs

---

1 ....

Superstitions about cats have existed for thousands of years. During the Middle Ages, people thought that cats had evil powers. People often burned cats to protect their homes from fire. They also believed that black cats were superhuman and worked with witches. Many black cats were killed during this period.

2 ....

Today, black cats are either a symbol of good luck or of bad luck. If a black cat crosses your path in England or Japan, it will bring you good luck. However, in America and most of Europe, it is very unlucky.

---

2 Read part of a text about Britain's unluckiest man. Match the correct heading (a–c) with the paragraphs (1–2).

   a Car crashes

   b Childhood accidents

   c Lucky to be alive

---

1 ....

When John Lynne was a child, he fell off a horse and was immediately run over by a van. When he was a teenager, he fell out of a tree and broke his arm. After several days in hospital, he went home on the bus. It was Friday, 13th. The bus crashed and he broke his arm again.

2 ....

As an adult, John Lynne has had about twelve serious accidents which nearly killed him. For example, he has been hit by lightning and by falling rocks in a mine. He has also been in three major road accidents.

Listening

3 🔘 2.3 Listen to the conversation. Which animal (a, b or c) are they talking about?

Word list Unit 2

association (n)	....	introvert (n)	....
attract (v)	....	invisible (adj)	....
avalanche (n)	....	ladder (n)	....
avoid (v)	....	leprechaun (n)	....
bad luck (n phr)	....	merrow (n)	....
be fed up (with sth) (phr v)	....	moody (adj)	....
		nocturnal (adj)	....
behaviour (n)	....	octopus pl octopuses (n)	....
bolt (n)	....	offend (v)	....
bonobo (n)	....	pathway (n)	....
bossy (adj)	....	pillow (n)	....
brain (n)	....	pollution (n)	....
brush (n)	....	pooka (n)	....
cage (n)	....	primate (n)	....
captivity (n)	....	protect (v)	....
common (adj)	....	recognise (v)	....
cormorant (n)	....	researcher (n)	....
count backwards (phr)	....	reward (n & v)	....
disappear (v)	....	ribbon (n)	....
earthquake (n)	....	sailor (n)	....
enclosure (n)	....	scary (adj)	....
encourage (v)	....	slaughterhouse (n)	....
escape (v)	....	sled (n)	....
evil (adj)	....	slideshow (n)	....
exploit (v)	....	sniff out (phr v)	....
extrovert (n/adj)	....	sociable (adj)	....
fairy (n)	....	stuck (adj)	....
fence (n)	....	superstition (n)	....
fix (v)	....	superstitious (adj)	....
four-leaf shamrock (n)	....	surgeon (n)	....
good luck (n phr)	....	sweat (n)	....
greedy (adj)	....	temporary (adj)	....
habit (n)	....	tool (n)	....
horseshoe (n)	....	trap (v)	....
instinct (n)	....	trick (n & v)	....
interpretation (n)	....	trunk (n)	....

present perfect continuous

We use the **present perfect continuous** to talk about a continuous activity which began in the past and has continued up to the present.

We form the present perfect continuous with *have/has been*, followed by the **present participle** of the main verb.

We form the negative with *haven't/ hasn't been*, followed by the present participle of the main verb.

We make questions by putting *have/has* before the subject and then *been*, followed by the present participle of the main verb.

In short answers we use *have/has* or *haven't/ hasn't*. We DON'T use *been* or the main verb.

present perfect continuous and present perfect simple

Notice that we use the **present perfect simple**, NOT the present perfect continuous – to talk about:

- a decision, conclusion, etc which is the result of a continuous activity
  I've been searching on the Internet and I've found some good sites.

- a state, thought or feeling, beginning in the past and continuing up to the present (see Unit 1: *verbs without a continuous form*)
  I've been watching this film for over an hour, but I haven't understood what it's about. (Not: *haven't been understanding*)

present perfect continuous with *for* and *since*

We use *for* with the present perfect continuous to talk about *duration*.

*I've been studying English **for four years**.*

We use *since* with the present perfect continuous for an activity which has continued up to the present, to talk about when it started. *Since* is followed by a time, date, year, etc, or a phrase that describes a particular time.

*I've been studying French **since 2009/since the age of eleven**.*

1 Circle the correct option.

I've (known)/ been knowing Jay for /(since) our first year at school.

1 We've *waited / been waiting* for a bus *for / since* half an hour.

2 Have you *seen / been seeing* the new Angelina Jolie film yet?

3 I've *applied / been applying* for summer jobs *for / since* March.

4 She's *written / been writing* this novel *for / since* last year.

5 He's always *believed / been believing* he'll be famous one day.

2 Complete the sentences. Use the present perfect simple or present perfect continuous form of the verbs in brackets.

I *'ve been tidying* (tidy) my room for almost an hour, so I *'ve decided* (decide) to take a break.

1 I .... (send) emails all day, but I .... (not have) a single reply yet.

2 Davy .... (do) research all day for his history project and now he .... (find) enough information to start writing.

3 The players .... (train) hard since the season started and the team's results .... (improve) a lot.

4 Sam and I .... (agree) to play a duet in the school concert, so we .... (practise) together for the last two weeks.

5 Karen .... (take) singing lessons for a couple of years and now she .... (enter) a national talent competition.

relative clauses

We can join two short sentences together by making the second sentence into a **relative clause**; the first sentence contains the main information and the relative clause gives further information.
Dolphins are highly intelligent creatures. They are mammals.

We join the two sentences by changing the pronoun (*They*) into a **relative pronoun** (*which*).
*Dolphins, **which are mammals**, are highly intelligent creatures.* (Not: *which they are mammals*)

defining and non-defining relative clauses

The meaning of the first sentence may be incomplete without the further information given in the relative clause. The relative clause defines the noun in the first sentence, so it is a **defining relative clause**.
People are afraid of spiders. (Which people?)
They have arachnophobia. (This defines which people we mean.)
*People **who have arachnophobia** are afraid of spiders.*

If the meaning of the first sentence is complete on its own, the relative clause doesn't define the noun in the first sentence. It simply gives extra information and so it is a **non-defining relative clause**.

Dolphins, __which are mammals__, are highly intelligent creatures.
With non-defining relative clauses we use commas before and after the relative clause, to separate the extra information from the main part of the sentence.

relative pronouns and relative adverbs

For **people**, we use *who*.
*People **who** have arachnophobia are afraid of spiders.*

For **animals/things**, we use *which*.
*A bonobo, **which** is a type of chimpanzee, is also very intelligent.*

For **people** and **animals/things**, we use *whose* to show possession.
*The chimpanzee, **whose** arm was broken, couldn't climb.*

For **times**, we use the relative adverb *when*.
*At 5.30, **when** most people are going home, there is heavy traffic.*

For **places**, we use the relative adverb *where*.
*The place **where** patients are treated is a hospital.*

In **defining** relative clauses, but not in non-defining relative clauses, we can use *that* instead of *who* or *which*.

3 **Complete the sentences with *who, which, whose, when* or *where*.**

The girl *who* spoke to us is Joe's cousin.

1 Kingston, ... reggae music began, is the capital of Jamaica.
2 Shakespeare, ... wrote so many famous plays, was also an actor.
3 At seven o'clock, ... Dad gets home from work, we have dinner.
4 Sheepdogs, ... are easy to train, make very good pets.
5 Ilse, ... parents are German, has never been to Germany.

4 **Join the sentences with *who, which* or *whose*. Use commas where necessary.**

The boy is a friend of mine. He lives here.

The boy who lives here is a friend of mine.

1 Pelé was the world's greatest footballer. His career ended in 1977.

....

2 The only person is my mum. She really understands me.

....

3 I think smoking should be banned. It's a dangerous habit.

....

4 The band members are close friends. They grew up together.

....

5 One thing is intelligence. It makes us different from other species.

....

question tags

Question tags are short questions added to the end of a statement. Question tags show that:

- the speaker expects the listener(s) to agree with the statement.
  Dolphins are mammals (statement), ***aren't they?*** (question tag)
  (The speaker expects the answer *Yes, they are*.)

- the speaker is not completely sure that the statement is correct and wants to check.
  You're not serious (statement), ***are you?*** (question tag)
  (The speaker is not completely sure and wants to check.)

We form a question tag with the same modal, auxiliary or form of *be* which is used in the statement, followed by the appropriate subject pronoun. We do not use a name or a noun phrase in the question tag.
*Frankie will help us, **won't he?*** (Not: *won't ~~Frankie~~?*)
*You and I are best friends, **aren't we?*** (Not: *aren't ~~you and I~~?*)

If the statement is affirmative, the question tag is negative. If the statement is negative, the question tag is affirmative.

*Joe **is** (affirmative) forgetful, **isn't** (negative) he?*
*You **haven't** (negative) lost your key again, **have** (affirmative) you?*

If there is no modal, auxiliary or form of *be* in the statement, we use ***don't/doesn't*** or ***did/didn't***.
*You remember Holly, **don't you?***

5 **Add question tags to the statements.**

Dogs are really intelligent animals, *aren't they*?

1 Christine's brother likes rap music, ...?
2 It's too late to call her, ...?
3 Penguins can't fly, ...?
4 You'll help me with my homework, ...?
5 Dogs and cats usually fight, ...?
6 It's the first time you've done this, ...?
7 You haven't forgotten already, ...?
8 Louise should phone her parents, ...?

Review Units 1 and 2

Grammar review: present simple and present continuous

1 **Complete the sentences with the correct form of the verbs in brackets.**

1 He usually .... (spend) one or two hours online every night.

2 I often listen to her records these days – I .... (become) a big fan of her music!

3 They .... (work) on a new album – I'm not sure when it will be finished.

4 She .... (sign) autographs when the fans ask her to. She thinks it's important.

5 Come and listen to this! Don't you think they .... (sing) out of tune?

1 mark per item: ...... / 5 marks

Present perfect simple and continuous

2 **Complete the sentences with the correct form of the verbs in brackets.**

1 Alison .... (never / be) to a live concert.

2 I'm really tired. I .... (work) in the garden all day.

3 It .... (rain) non-stop for three days!

4 My mum .... (always / have) long hair.

5 Sorry I'm late. How long .... (you / wait)?

1 mark per item: ...... / 5 marks

3 **Complete the dialogue with the present simple or continuous or the present perfect simple or continuous form of the verbs in brackets.**

Jess: Look! The celebrities [1]..................... (start) to arrive at the theatre for the film première.

Paul: Yes. I [2]..................... (think) that's Leo DiCaprio over there. He [3]..................... (get) out of the car and now he [4]..................... (wave) to the crowd.

Jess: Oh yes. Who [5]..................... (he / hold) hands with? I [6]..................... (never / see) her before. She [7]..................... (look) amazing!

Paul: That's his new girlfriend. He [8]..................... (not go out) with her for long. She [9]..................... (not be) a celebrity, so that's probably why you [10]..................... (not recognise) her.

2 marks per item: ...... / 20 marks

Still, yet, already and just

4 **Put the words in the correct order to make statements and questions.**

1 we / heard / have / the / just / about / accident.

....

2 have / the / told / yet / about / you / fans / it / ?

....

3 yes, / stopped / tonight's / we've / already / show.

....

4 hurry up! / has / arrived. / just / taxi / The

....

5 is / putting on / she / still / make-up / her / ?

....

1 mark per item: ...... / 5 marks

Relative clauses

5 **Join each pair of sentences to make one sentence. Use the relative pronouns in the box.**

when	where	which	who	whose

1 Stratford-upon-Avon is very popular with tourists. Shakespeare lived there.

....

2 New York is known as the city that never sleeps. It is on the east coast of America.

....

3 Buddy Holly died in a plane crash. He was a singer.

....

4 Spring time is the worst time for allergies. There is a lot of pollen then.

....

5 Ian McEwan is my favourite author. His latest book has been made into a film.

....

2 marks per item: ...... / 10 marks

Question tags

6 **Complete the checking questions with a question tag.**

1 They haven't arrived yet, ...?

2 You're at Tim's party, ...?

3 Sue isn't a very good dancer, ...?

4 You don't know where my mobile is, ...?

5 He hasn't forgotten my book again, ...?

1 mark per item: ...... / 5 marks

Vocabulary review: mass media

7 **Circle the odd word out.**

1 article   headline   viewers
2 audition   repeat   rehearsal
3 channel   listeners   station
4 soap opera   judge   episode
5 journalist   reporter   DJ

1 mark per item: ...... / 5 marks

Personality and the mind

8 **Complete the sentences with the correct verbs.**

1 I can't r...................... much about what happened.
2 We all found it hard to u...................... Einstein's theories.
3 If you f...................... lonely, just send me a text and I'll come and see you.
4 It is difficult to t...................... about abstract ideas.
5 Can you i...................... what aliens from another planet would look like?

1 mark per item: ...... / 5 marks

9 **Choose the correct word.**

| ambition   creativity   fear   funny   imaginative |
| introvert   logical   memory   moody   sociable |

1 A phobia is a strong .... of something, such as snakes, spiders or water.
2 Julie's .... is to be a TV journalist.
3 You need to have a high level of .... to work in advertising – it's all about ideas.
4 Sometimes jokes aren't .... if you try to translate them.
5 Teenagers are often .... because they are going through a lot of change in their lives.
6 Tim is a(n) .... – he is quite shy and prefers his own company.
7 She's always making up stories – she's a very .... child.
8 To be a good chess player, you need a very clear and .... mind.
9 Dogs are very .... and need the company of humans or other animals.
10 Our .... often gets weaker as we get older – we retain less and forget more.

1 mark per item: ...... / 10 marks

Prepositions

10 **Complete the sentence with the correct prepositions.**

1 Don't look directly .... the sun. It's dangerous.
2 I'm not very good .... singing.
3 Debra tried .... about six pairs of jeans.
4 Can you turn the sound .... on the TV? I'm trying to sleep.
5 There's a good film .... TV tonight.
6 Did you find .... what time the show starts?
7 Are you afraid .... spiders?
8 The children couldn't play outside because .... the bad weather.
9 You're not listening .... a word I'm saying!
10 I like staying .... home and watching TV.

1 mark per item: ...... / 10 marks

Communicate

11 **Match the responses (a–e) to the statements and questions (1–5).**

a Yes, it's great, isn't it?   **b** I know what you mean.
c No, I haven't.   **d** He seems a bit moody to me.
e Because it's very exciting.

1 You haven't seen the film *Avatar*, have you? ☐
2 Why do you say that? ☐
3 I don't like our new maths teacher – she always seems to be in a bad mood! ☐
4 *Cats* is a great musical – the best ever! ☐
5 What do you think of Jack? ☐

2 marks per item: ...... / 10 marks

12 **Complete the paragraph with the words in the box.**

| appear   episode   for   had   have |
| of   viewers   when   where   which |

What do celebrities do [1]...................... they're not famous any more? In Britain, the answer is easy: they [2]...................... on *I'm a Celebrity – Get Me Out Of Here!* This is a reality TV show [3]...................... can help celebrities to start their careers again. Twelve celebrities are put in the jungle, [4]...................... they have to survive together [5]...................... three weeks. To get food, they have to do special tests involving insects and other creatures. In the last [6]......................, one celebrity [7]...................... to sit in a tank of snakes. Although she was afraid [8]...................... them, she performed the task really well. Each week, around 9 million [9]...................... watch the programme. Celebrities who [10]...................... been in the show include Joe Bugner and Martina Navratilova.

1 mark per item: ...... / 10 marks

Total marks: ...... / 100

3A Digging up the past

Vocabulary: time

1 Answer the quiz questions.

Quiz

What 't' do busy people need more of?

time

1 Which word beginning with 'm' means one thousand years?

....

2 Which 'd' refers to a period of ten years?

....

3 Which 'f' means fourteen nights or two weeks?

....

4 Which 'm' is smaller than an hour, but bigger than a second?

....

5 Which 'y' has 52 weeks in it?

....

6 Which 'm' consists of approximately 30 days?

....

7 Which 'c' refers to one hundred years?

....

8 Which 'h' has 3,600 seconds in it?

....

2 Complete the paragraphs with words from Exercise 1. Use the plural form where necessary.

1 I think that the 1960s was one of the most exciting ¹..................... of the twentieth ²..................... . Important changes took place during this ³..................... . For example, women began to have more freedom in their lives.

2 It's amazing to think that only 20 ⁴..................... ago, most people didn't have a computer at home. However, since the beginning of the new ⁵....................., technology has become part of most people's lives. Nowadays, children and adults spend at least two ⁶..................... a day in front of their computers.

Vocabulary: archaeology

3 Look at the pictures and complete the captions.

1 Roman ....

2 a ....

3 a pile of ....

4 the .... of a Greek temple

5 an archaeological ....

4 Complete the texts with the words in the box. There is one extra word.

> archaeologists artefacts document fragment
> jewellery palaeontologists remains

¹..................... are things which were used by humans in the past. Examples include pots, tools and ²..................... . Experts, called ³....................., carefully dig them up and study them to learn about life in ancient times. Sometimes they only find broken pieces of something, but even the smallest ⁴..................... can provide a lot of information.

⁵................... study prehistoric life. They try to describe and explain what happened in the past. They use evidence from nature to develop theories. This evidence often includes the frozen ⁶..................... of prehistoric animals.

Grammar: past perfect

5 Put the events (a–g) in the correct order.

.... **a** In the morning, a loud noise woke him up really early.

.... **b** By the time he got to school, he was prepared for the exam, but he was too tired to answer any of the questions!

......*1*..... **c** Ben fell asleep in the middle of his science exam yesterday.

.... **d** He couldn't go back to sleep, so he got up and studied some more.

.... **e** This is because he'd stayed up late the night before to study.

.... **f** Even after he'd gone to bed, he stayed awake studying until after midnight.

.... **g** Some workmen had started digging up the road.

6 Match the beginnings of the sentences (1–6) with the endings (a–f).

1 When Mary opened her bag, ...*b*.....

2 My grandparents had only known each other for a month ....

3 Jack and Diane had never met ....

4 When we got to the cinema, ...

5 The children knew a lot about animals ....

6 They couldn't see the play ....

a before they got married.

b she realised she'd left her money at home.

c because they'd grown up on a farm.

d before last night.

e because the tickets had sold out.

f the film had already started.

7 Complete the text with the past simple or past perfect form of the verbs in brackets.

Caitlin *had never visited* (never / visit) the British Museum before, so it was the first time she ¹ .... (ever / see) artefacts from so many different places! She ² .... (think) that the Egyptian statues and sculptures in Room Four ³ .... (be) really fascinating! After she ⁴ .... (look) at the enormous sculptures, she ⁵ .... (go) into another room. There were many artefacts there, which archaeologists ⁶ .... (bring) back from Egypt at the beginning of the last century. There was a collection of mummies, which the Ancient Egyptians .... (put) inside beautiful tombs before closing them up inside the Pyramids. During the 19th century, European explorers ⁸ .... (take) the mummies from their tombs and ⁹ .... (sell) them to museums back home. In Caitlin's opinion, the Egyptologists ¹⁰ .... (steal) the mummies. This ¹¹ .... (make) her feel sad, so she ¹² .... (decide) to leave the room and find something else to look at.

Working with words: verb + *to* + infinitive

8 Complete the dialogue with the correct form of the verbs in the box.

agree	not wait	~~come~~	like
not need	prefer	try	want

Lisa: Hi, Katie. I'*m coming* to stay next weekend if that's OK with you.

Katie: Fantastic! Are you coming by bus?

Lisa: Actually, I ¹ .... to travel by train. I ² .... to buy a ticket online this afternoon, but their website wasn't working. Anyway, I ³ .... to see you again!

Katie: Me neither! What would you ⁴ .... to do when you get here?

Lisa: Well, I ⁵ .... to buy a new jacket, so perhaps we could go shopping.

Katie: Good idea! Let's go to the big shopping centre just outside town.

Lisa: Yeah. Great! We can catch the bus there, can't we?

Katie: We ⁶ .... to do that! I'm sure my mum will ⁷ .... to drive us there if I ask her nicely.

9 Complete the sentences with the correct form of the verbs in brackets.

1 The film was really boring, so we .... (decide / leave).

2 She was so angry that she .... (refuse / talk) to anyone for nearly a week!

3 After six attempts, he finally .... (manage / pass) his driving test.

4 How old were you when you .... (learn / swim)?

5 Ben .... (hope / study) archaeology at university next year.

6 My dog .... (seem / understand) everything I say to her.

7 My dad .... (not learn / cook) when he was young.

Reading

1 Look at the pictures and read the text quickly. Match the diary entries (1–2) with the pictures (a–c). There is one extra picture.

Being a teenager in the 1980s

by Kara Williams

My mum's name is Diane. She grew up during the '80s, before the time of home computers, DVDs and the Internet. Here are some extracts from her diary, which I think give a good idea of what life was like then.

1 ....

Saturday, 16 August

I've just got back from a party at Janine's and it was brilliant! I wore my new rah-rah skirt, legwarmers and a white blouse with lots of frills. I went over to Janine's house at about 7 o'clock. Her parents had gone out that morning for the whole day, so we had the house to ourselves. Janine and her older brother, Steve, had set up a disco in the garage. All Steve's friends play in a band together. Steve plays the synthesiser. They were all wearing lots of black eye-liner and had long geometric fringes! Anyway, the music was great. They played lots of my favourite music – Spandau Ballet, Depeche Mode and Boy George. I danced for ages, then went to get a drink from the kitchen. Steve and his friends were next door in the living room watching a video they'd rented. It was called Teen Wolf. I'd never seen it before, so I sat down to watch it for a while. We all thought it was a bit boring and Steve started making jokes about it. Steve's really

funny and he's good-looking too. I really like him!

2 ....

Sunday, 17 August

Today was really boring, but I couldn't stop thinking about Steve. We went to Grandma's house for lunch. We came home at about 5 o'clock and I helped Mum with the Sunday roast – I peeled the potatoes and chopped the vegetables and Mum prepared the meat. After we had eaten dinner, Annie and I washed the dishes and listened to the Top 20 on the radio. Then I went to do my homework in my bedroom. I had just finished and I was going to start listening to my new Yazoo cassette when the phone rang in the hall. It was Melanie – she'd had an argument with her boyfriend. She was upset and talked for ages! After that, I went into the living room to watch TV, but my favourite programme had nearly finished. In the end, I went to bed early and read my book.

2 Read the first diary entry again and put the events in the correct order.

.... **a** Diane went to Janine's house.

.... **b** Janine's parents went out.

.... **c** Diane decided to get a drink.

.... **d** Janine and Steve set up the disco in the garage.

.... **e** Diane joined Steve and his friends in the living room.

.... **f** Steve made funny jokes about the film.

.... **g** Diane danced to her favourite music.

3 Read the second diary entry and complete the summarising sentences.

1 Diane and her family visited their grandmother
....

2 Diane helped her mum to ....
....

3 After dinner, Diane and her sister, Annie, did
....

4 The phone rang before Diane ....
....

5 Diane went into the hall to ....
....

6 Melanie was upset because ....
....

7 Diane went to the living room to watch TV, but ....

Listening

4 Look at the photos (a–c) of technological gadgets from the 1980s. Choose the best caption (1–3) for each photo.

1 The coolest gadget at the time was a personal stereo called the Sony Walkman. ....

2 Smaller mobile phones did not appear until much later. ....

3 Radio-cassette players were large and heavy. ....

5 **3.1** Now listen to three British people talking about gadgets in the 1980s. Match the speakers (1–3) with the photos (a–c).

1 ....
2 ....
3 ....

b

a

c

6 Listen again. Circle the correct answers.

1 Where did Mike first see a mobile phone?
a in a pub
b in a film
c in the street

2 What is his opinion of them now?
a He thinks they look cool.
b He thinks they're ordinary.
c He is still excited by them.

3 Where did Lenny and his friends use to play their music?
a outside in parks or on the street
b on the beach
c in poor neighbourhoods

4 When did Judy use to listen to her personal stereo?
a when she was travelling
b while she was studying
c while she was shopping

5 Which gadgets used to annoy other people?
a mobile phones and personal stereos
b personal stereos and radio-cassette players
c radio-cassette players and mobile phones

Grammar: *used to*

7 Complete the dialogues with *used to* or the past simple. Use *used to* whenever possible.

1

A: ^{1} .... (you / stay) for school dinners when you were a kid?

B: No, I didn't. I ^{2} .... (go) home for lunch. I only ^{3} .... (have) a school dinner once and I ^{4} .... (hate) it!

2

A: We ^{5} .... (not go) abroad on holiday when I was a kid. We ^{6} .... (visit) my aunts and uncles in Wales. What about you?

B: We ^{7} .... (go) camping in the south of France with another family. We always ^{8} .... (stay) at the same campsite. One year, we ^{9} .... (decide) to do something different, so we ^{10} .... (hire) a house boat instead.

3C Talking about quantity

Useful expressions

1 Complete the dialogues with the correct form of the verbs in the box.

| feel | look | ~~look~~ | smell | sound | taste |

1

Assistant: Those jeans *look* great on you!

Customer: Do you think so? Actually, they
¹....................... a bit tight. Have you
got a larger size?

2

Boy: Hey, Mum! What happened to the cake?
It ²....................... really funny.

Mum: I know. I'm afraid it sank in the middle,
but it still ³....................... good. Try some!

3

Student: Ugh! It ⁴....................... awful in here!

Teacher: I know. We've been doing experiments
with chemicals this afternoon.

Student: That ⁵....................... cool! Can we do
some too?

2 Match the question words (1–6) with the
endings (a–f).

1 How far   **a** did the train leave?

2 How long   **b** did you become a teacher?

3 How many   **c** does it cost to fly to America?

4 How much   **d** does it take to make a cake?

5 What time   **e** knives do we need?

6 When   **f** is the bus station from here?

3 🔊 **3.2** Listen to the questions and choose the
best answer (a or b).

1 a tomorrow morning   **b** at half past two

2 a this afternoon   **b** ten minutes

3 a an hour and a half   **b** at ten o'clock

4 a more than £25   **b** about half an hour

5 a four days   **b** two kilometres

6 a about four kilos   **b** usually six

4 Complete the dialogue with the words and
expressions in the box.

| feels | how far | how long |
| how much | look | ~~smells~~ | sounds |

Kara: Hi, Jen. Come in.

Jen: Hi, Kara. Mmm! Something *smells* good!

Kara: Yeah. Mum's making Bolognese sauce.
Shall we go upstairs and check our
Facebook pages?

Jen: OK. But I'd like to say hi to your mum
first. Hi, Mrs Williams.

Mum: Hi, Jen. You ¹....................... nice. Is that a
new jacket?

Jen: Actually, it's quite old.

Kara: Really? I've never seen it before.
²....................... have you had it?

Jen: About six months, I think.

Kara: What's it made of? It ³....................... really
soft.

Jen: I think it's made of leather.

Kara: Really? ⁴....................... did it cost?

Jen: Actually, I only paid £35 for it. I got it from
the second-hand market in Donnington.
It's an amazing place. It's open every day
from early in the morning until about
6 p.m. and they sell all sorts of things.

Mum: Second-hand market? That ⁵.......................
fun. ⁶....................... is it to Donnington?

Jen: I'm not sure. But it only takes 30 minutes
by car.

Mum: Shall we go this weekend, Kara?

Kara: Yeah. Great idea! Thanks, Mum.

Pronunciation: words containing *ui*

5 **Read the sentences. How do you pronounce the underlined words?**

1 There was a <u>quiz</u> on the <u>cruise</u> ship every night.

2 The neighbours in our <u>building</u> are <u>quite</u> <u>quiet</u>.

3 A <u>guide</u> showed us round the <u>ruins</u>.

4 We stopped for a <u>quick</u> drink in a bar.

5 I have orange <u>juice</u> and <u>biscuits</u> every morning.

6 The doctor told me to drink plenty of <u>liquids</u> and eat more <u>fruit</u>.

6 🔊 **3.3** **Now listen and check. Practise saying the sentences.**

Writing: a recommendation

7 **Read Kara's comments about the Style Café. Complete the text with the adjectives in the box.**

| artistic | busy | colourful | cool | delicious | enjoyable |
| excellent | expensive | friendly | ~~popular~~ | | |

000

Student Guide
Where to eat

I went to the Style Café last Saturday with three of my friends. It's very *popular* at the moment because it's only just opened and everyone wants to go there. We had to wait to get a table. Inside, the café is an interesting place. The decoration is modern and very bright and ¹..................... – everything is brilliant red and purple. There are lots of pictures as well as ²..................... black-and-white photographs on all the walls. The music was great. They played tracks by ³..................... artists such as Coldplay and The Jonas Brothers. Eventually, we got a table and a menu and we ordered cheeseburgers and chips. Our waitress was ⁴..................... and smiling and the service was ⁵..................... – the food arrived quickly and was nice and hot. The burger tasted ⁶..................... and the chips were fantastic. The food was probably a bit more ⁷..................... than other cafés in the area, but we had such a(n) ⁸..................... time that we didn't really mind. I can recommend the Style Café to anyone, but I don't recommend going on a(n) ⁹..................... Saturday afternoon.

8 **Match the adjectives (1–6) with opposite adjectives from Exercise 7. There may be more than one possible answer.**

1 boring ....   **4** quiet ....

2 cheap ....   **5** tasteless ....

3 dull ....   **6** terrible ....

9 **Complete the second sentence with the word in brackets so that it means the same as the first.**

The café was so new that everyone wanted to go there. (such)

It was such a new café that everyone wanted to go there.

1 The café was so busy that we couldn't get a table. (such)

It .... that we couldn't get a table.

2 It had such great pictures on the walls that we didn't mind waiting. (so)

The pictures on .... that we didn't mind waiting.

3 The waitress was so good that our food arrived within ten minutes. (such)

She .... that our food arrived within ten minutes.

4 The burger was so tasty that I ate it all. (such)

It .... I ate it all.

5 It was such a large portion of chips that we couldn't finish it. (so)

The portion of .... we couldn't finish it.

10 **Make notes about a café or restaurant you have been to recently.**

The place

....

The music

....

The decoration

....

The service

....

The food

....

The price

....

Would you recommend it? Why / Why not?

....

11 **Now write a short text for a magazine about 'Places to eat in my town'. Include the information in your notes in Exercise 10. Begin by saying when you ate at this place and who you were with.**

Reading

1 Choose the description (1–3) which matches the picture.

> 1
> My great-grandfather worked at the natural history museum as an archaeologist. He used to go on archaeological digs with other archaeologists. He sometimes took my grandmother with him and she helped to look for artefacts. They used to travel by bus and stayed in tents near the site.

> 2
> When my grandmother was a young woman, she used to go abroad with her father, who was an archaeologist. They often visited sites in South America and Egypt. They used to hire a car and travel around looking for old remains and artefacts, which they cleaned and took home with them.

> 3
> When she was younger, my grandmother used to visit archaeological sites all around the world. She used to go on organised trips to places like Peru and Egypt. Sometimes the archaeologists used to let her stay and help with the digging.

Listening

2 🔘 **3.4** Listen and match the conversations (1–3) with the places (a–d). There is one extra place.

1 ....   **a** a museum
2 ....   **b** a market
3 ....   **c** a restaurant
            d a zoo

3 🔘 **3.5** Listen and match the conversations (1–3) with the places (a–d). There is one extra place.

1 ....   **a** a shop
2 ....   **b** a farm
3 ....   **c** a street
            d a restaurant

Word list Unit 3

afterwards (adv)	....		last (v)	....
artefact (n)	....		legwarmers (n pl)	....
bake (v)	....		length (n)	....
baking soda (n)	....		mammoth (n)	....
baking tray (n)	....		mud (n)	....
base (on) (v)	....		oven (n)	....
bitter (adj)	....		palaeontologist (n)	....
boil (v)	....		pavement (n)	....
bone (n)	....		peel (v)	....
celebration (n)	....		plant (n)	....
childhood (n)	....		pottery (n)	....
chop (v)	....		preserve (v)	....
combine (v)	....		provide (v)	....
corn (n)	....		quantity (n)	....
cornbread (n)	....		recipe (n)	....
crop (n)	....		remains (n pl)	....
disgusting (adj)	....		revolting (adj)	....
display (n)	....		robber (n)	....
elevator (US) (n)	....		rubbish tip (n)	....
equal (v)	....		ruins (n pl)	....
evidence (n)	....		run out (of) (phr v)	....
examine (v)	....		share (v)	....
feast (n)	....		shop keeper (n)	....
fossil (n)	....		significant (adj)	....
frill (n)	....		site (n)	....
fringe (n)	....		snowmobile (n)	....
frozen (adj)	....		squash (n)	....
fry (v)	....		steak and kidney pie (n)	....
get trapped (v)	....		thaw (v)	....
guidebook (n)	....		temple (n)	....
harvest (n)	....		tomb (n)	....
heat up (v)	....		turkey (n)	....
herder (n)	....		valuable (adj)	....
honestly (adv)	....		village (n)	....
horrify (v)	....		wooden (adj)	....
hunt (v)	....		wrap (v)	....
in honour of (phr)	....			

past perfect

We use the **past perfect** to talk about an action/event that happened at some time before another action, event or time in the past. Exactly when the earlier action/event happened is usually not mentioned.

*By 1920, World War I **had already ended**.*

We can present the two actions/events in any order, but we must use the past perfect for the one which happened first.

*Aborigines **had lived** in Australia for thousands of years by the time the first European people arrived.*
*By the time the first European people arrived, Aborigines **had lived** in Australia for thousands of years.*

We form the past perfect with **had/hadn't** + **past participle** of the main verb. It has the same form for all subjects (*I*, *he*, *we*, etc).

We form questions in the past perfect by putting **had** before the subject, followed by the past participle of the main verb.

1 **Complete the sentences and questions with the past perfect form of the verbs in brackets.**

By the end of the 1960s, astronauts *had landed* (land) on the moon.

1 When Nelson Mandela was released in 1990, he .... (be) a political prisoner for 27 years.

2 .... (the Inca empire / already / disappear) before the arrival of the Spanish conquistadors?

3 By the middle of the Industrial Revolution, millions of people .... (move) from the countryside to the cities in search of work.

4 .... (any Europeans / travel) to China before Marco Polo went there?

2 **Complete the sentences with the past simple or past perfect form of the verbs in brackets. The verbs are given in the order in which the events happened.**

I couldn't believe it when I *heard* that I *had won* first prize. (1: win, 2: hear)

1 The film .... by the time we .... to the cinema. (1: already / start, 2: get)

2 My favourite childhood toy .... a doll which my gran .... for my mum. (1: make, 2: be)

3 Experts quickly .... what .... the plane to crash. (1: cause, 2: discover)

4 We .... from our holiday to find that a burglar .... the flat. (1: break into, 2: return)

5 By the time the boy's mother .... reading him a bedtime story, he .... asleep. (1: fall, 2: finish)

3 **Complete the sentences with the past simple or past perfect form of the verbs in brackets.**

He *was* (be) worried about the test because he *hadn't studied* (not study) for it.

1 Yesterday I .... (find) a wallet that someone .... (leave) on the bus.

2 Columbus .... (reach) America several centuries after the Vikings .... (sail) across the Atlantic.

3 Karim .... (never / see) snow until the first time he .... (visit) Europe.

4 Police cars .... (rush) to the scene, but the bank robbers .... (already / make) their getaway.

used to

We can use **used to** for:

- past habits or states that are now finished
*I **used to read** Superhero comics. (I don't now.)*
*People **used to think** the plague was carried in the air. (Now we know it isn't.)*

- things that existed or often happened in the past, but do not exist/happen now.
*There **used to be** a field here. (Now there's a supermarket.)*

The form is **used to** + **bare infinitive** of the main verb for all subjects (*I, you, he*, etc).

We form the negative with **didn't** + **use to** + **bare infinitive** of the main verb.

*People **didn't use to have** computers. (Now they do.)*

We form questions with **did** + **subject** + **use to** + **bare infinitive** of the main verb.

***Did** she **use to work** in a bookshop? (She works in a bank now.)*

4 **Circle the correct option**

I used to (be)/ *being* afraid of insects when I (was)/ *used to be* a child.

1 *Did / Were* people use to *make / made* their own bread?

2 We *weren't used / didn't use* to *have / had* 3D films.

3 Computers *used / did use* to be bigger than they *are / use* now.

4 There *hadn't / didn't* use to *have / be* MP3 players twenty years ago.

5 What *did / were* people use to do before they *have / had* cars?

5 Rewrite the sentences and questions.

People used to believe that the Sun revolves around the Earth. (?)

Did people use to believe that the Sun revolves around the Earth?

1 Did India use to be part of the British Empire? (✓)

....

2 People didn't use to send emails in those days. (?)

....

3 Did most people use to eat healthily in the 1950s? (✗)

....

4 Books used to be copied by hand before printing was invented. (?)

....

5 Did people use to worry about ecology as much as we do now? (✗)

....

6 Write sentences. Use the correct form of *used to* where appropriate.

people / travel / on horseback in the 19th century?

Did people use to travel on horseback in the 19th century?

1 People / not have / mobile phones when my parents / be / teenagers.

....

2 I / eat / a lot of sweets, but now I / be / on a diet.

....

3 There / be / a farm where the golf course / be / now.

....

4 What sort of clothes / you / wear / when you / be / young, Dad?

....

result clauses

Result clauses are used in sentences which first describe a situation and then say what happened/happens/will happen as a result of this situation. The result clause joins the situation and the result in a single sentence.

Situation: *The food was spicy.*
Result: *We couldn't eat it.*
The food was **so spicy that** *we couldn't eat it.*

We form result clauses with *so* + **adjective** + *that* ... or *such* (*a/an*) + **adjective** + **noun** + *that* ... .
The food was **spicy**. (adjective)
The food was **so spicy** *that we couldn't eat it.*
It was a very **spicy meal**. (adjective + countable noun)
It was **such a spicy meal** *that we couldn't eat it.*
It was very **spicy food**. (adjective + uncountable noun)
It was **such spicy food** *that we didn't like it.*

We can also form result clauses with *so many* + **plural noun** or *so much* + **uncountable noun**.
There were **so many people** (plural) *at the museum* **that** *we couldn't see the displays.*
There was **so much noise** (uncountable) *that we couldn't hear the guide.*

7 Join the sentences. Use the words in brackets.

This is an exciting book. I can't put it down! (such)

This is such an exciting book that I can't put it down!

1 We were having fun. We didn't want to stop. (so much)

....

2 My dad's a careful driver. He's never had a crash. (such)

....

3 This food is delicious. I'd like a second helping, please. (so)

....

4 There were people there. We had to queue for hours. (so many)

....

5 It was great news. Erica was crying with happiness. (such)

....

4A Sporting success

Vocabulary: jobs

1 Match the statements (1–7) with the professions (a–g).

a secretary ....
b designer ....
c engineer ....
d lawyer ....
e mechanic ....
f paramedic ....
g actor ....

1 I'm going to an audition this afternoon for a part in a new play.

2 We won't be able to fix your car until tomorrow, I'm afraid.

3 Don't worry. I'm going to prove that you are innocent.

4 He's still alive! Let's get him into the ambulance and I'll give him some oxygen.

5 I think my latest collection will sell really well. People will love the colours and the materials I've used.

6 I'm a bit bored with my job. I spend all day working on the computer and organising my boss's diary.

7 We're designing a new car engine that will run on water, not petrol.

2 Complete the sentences with six more jobs.

1 A(n) .... connects the power supply to people's houses.
2 A(n) .... needs to be creative and enjoy working long hours in a hot kitchen.
3 A(n) .... manages money for a business or for people. He or she needs to enjoy working with numbers.
4 A(n) .... organises other people's work and makes sure things are done on time.
5 A(n) .... works for the army and fights when there is a war.
6 A(n) .... deals with letters and parcels.

Vocabulary: sports

3 Circle the correct option to complete the text.

Weekend sports

It has been an exciting weekend in the world of sport. In the athletics championships yesterday, British athlete John Alwanga *won / set /(broke)* the existing world record for the 100 metres. However, the Kenyans have [1] *won / got / beaten* most of the medals including the women's 200 and 400 metres, the long jump and the high jump. Irish gymnast Aisling Murphy [2] *won / scored / did* a perfect ten on the floor this morning. Let's see if she can do the same on the asymmetric bars tomorrow.

In football, Manchester [3] *hit / beat / won* Liverpool 2:1. Mark Corner [4] *made / marked / scored* both goals for his team. Liverpool's Wayne Jinx [5] *missed / lost / left* an opportunity to make it a 2:2 draw in the last minute. Liverpool are having a lot of bad luck this season and have [6] *broken / missed / lost* every game so far!

4 Complete the texts with the words in the box.

> coach physiotherapist player referee
> ring sponsors' stadium umpires

A Boxing is a very tough sport. Every boxer needs a good manager as well as a good ¹....................., who can teach him (or her) all the skills they need to survive in the  ²..................... . During a match, it is important that the ³..................... knows when to stop a fight if one of the boxers is in danger of serious injury. Boxing is hard on the body and boxers often employ a(n) ⁴..................... to massage their muscles and to help them recover after an injury.

B Tennis is a very competitive sport, but a(n) ¹..................... can earn a lot of prize money if they win a big tournament. Top tennis stars are also paid a lot for advertising their ²..................... products. One of the biggest events of the tennis year is the US Open tennis tournament. This takes place in a large ³..................... in Flushing Meadows Park in New York. All the top tennis stars compete and the ⁴....................., whose decision is final, are the best in the world.

Working with words: adjective + *to* + infinitive

5 Match the sentences (1–6) with the responses (a–g) to complete the dialogues. There is one extra response.

1 Colin is leaving the team next week. ☐
2 We stood by the road at the rally last weekend. ☐
3 The match was brilliant yesterday, wasn't it? ☐
4 Are there lots of spiders in your tent? ☐
5 The final is tomorrow. Shall we go? ☐
6 A wild boar ran across the road in front of my car! ☐

a Really? It's unusual to see one at this time of year.
b Isn't it dangerous to get so close?
c I think it'll be impossible to get tickets now.
d Yes, it was very exciting to watch.
e We'll be very sad to see him go.
f It was very hard to say goodbye.
g Yes. I found one in my hair this morning!

Grammar: the future

6 Look at the pictures. Write predictions based on the situation now.

1 The diver ....
....
....
....
....
....

2 The athlete ....
....
....
....
....
....

3 The ball ....
....
....
....
....
....

4 The driver ....
....
....
....
....
....

5 The scorekeeper ...
....
....
....
....
....

6 The swimmer ....
....
....
....
....
....

4B Designing the future

Listening

1 **4.1** Listen to two teenagers talking about jackets. Which jacket are they talking about? Choose the correct picture (a or b).

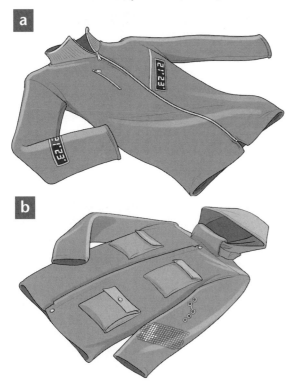

a

b

2 Listen again and choose the correct option (a, b or c).

1 The 'Bionic Jacket' is made of .... material.
   a thick
   b light
   c heavy

2 In cold weather, the material will
   a grow thicker.
   b grow longer.
   c grow extra parts.

3 In warm temperatures, the jacket will
   a be too uncomfortable.
   b get shorter.
   c cool down.

4 There is a small computer
   a inside the jacket.
   b on the sleeve.
   c on the hood.

5 Skiers who wear the jacket can check ....
   on a small screen.
   a their speed
   b their body temperature
   c the weather forecast

Vocabulary: clothes

3 **Circle the incorrect option.**

1 a *short-sleeved / bright yellow / cotton* skirt
2 a pair of *striped / V-neck / pastel* shorts
3 a *hooded / short-sleeved / patterned* dress
4 a pair of *tight / striped / round-neck* trousers
5 a pair of *flared / long-sleeved / denim* jeans

Grammar: future continuous

4 **Complete the sentences with the future continuous form of the verbs in the box.**

compete	do	~~lie~~	not use	start	wear	work

This time next week, I'*ll be lying* on the beach in the hot sun.

1 Fashionable skiers .... the 'Bionic Jacket' on the slopes next year.

2 This time tomorrow, I .... in the athletics championships.

3 Twenty years from now, we .... washing machines anymore.

4 By the time I'm twenty, I .... for a famous fashion designer.

5 A: What exam .... you .... this time next week?
   B: None! Next Monday, I .... my new job as a mechanic.

5 **Write one word in each gap to complete the email.**

To: Everyone
Subject: The future!
Hi,

I found some predictions from the 1920s and 1930s, which I thought were quite funny. This is what the 'experts' said back then:

In fifty years [1]...................... now, nobody will travel by car anymore. They will shoot down tubes instead.

[2]...................... 2020, men will [3]...................... wearing shorts for every occasion except formal events.

In forty years' [4]......................, two-thirds of babies will develop in laboratories.

This time next century, most people will only work fifteen hours a week.

So, what do you think? [5]...................... any of these predictions come true? I certainly hope that I [6]...................... be working less than 15 hours a week!

Lou

Reading

6 Read the article and match the headings (a–d) with the paragraphs (1–3). There is one extra heading.

a Clever clothes

b Invisible clothes

c Clothes in a can

d Bye-bye washing machine!

Sci-fi clothing

What will people be wearing in five, ten or twenty years from now? Will clothes look much the same as they do today or will they resemble something from a science fiction novel? Scroll down to find out more about the latest uses of technology in clothes design.

1 ....

It may sound like an idea from a science-fiction novel, but spray-on clothes have already been invented. In 2007, Manul Torres, a student at the Royal College of Art in London, developed a *fabric* that comes in a spray can. He called his invention 'Fabrican' and it can be used to create skin-tight tops and dresses. Although the product is already available to buy, will people actually wear it? Fabrican clothing is very thin and does not provide much cover or warmth. Until someone invents a thicker version, fashion models will probably be the only people to use it.

2 ....

Nanotechnology will be the next big thing in fashion design. Fabrics are treated with nanoparticles to give them special qualities. These particles are invisible to the eye and are already used to make clothes and footwear that *are waterproof* and don't *stain*. Liquid that touches the surface simply forms a bead and rolls off. Sportswear has already been designed which takes sweat away from the body and onto the outside of the clothing. Chemicals can also be added to the fabric which will stop bacteria from growing. Soldiers in the United States army have already tested the technology while fighting in the Middle East. They wore the same undershirts for many weeks, but found that they didn't get dirty!

3 ....

Dresses that change colour with your *mood*? This probably seems like an idea straight out of *Star Trek*. However, 'Smart Clothes' are tomorrow's street fashion. Thanks to advances in LED (light-emitting diode) technology, it will soon be possible to produce electronic lights and screens which will be light enough to wear as part of your clothing. Sensors will cause lights to change colour each time your *mood* changes. Smart Clothes will also allow you to change the patterns and designs on your clothes *whenever you like*. If you get bored with the design on your T-shirt, all you will need to do is download an image from the Internet and onto an invisible screen.

7 Read the text again. Are the sentences true or false?

	T	F
1 It will not be possible to buy Fabrican until next year.	☐	☐
2 The writer believes that everyone will soon be wearing spray-on clothes.	☐	☐
3 American soldiers have tested uniforms which use nanotechnology.	☐	☐
4 Some nanotechnology clothes can kill bacteria.	☐	☐
5 Clothes with electronic lights and screens in them are already available.	☐	☐
6 The patterns on Smart Clothes change automatically when your mood changes.	☐	☐
7 In the future, you will be able to download clothes from the Internet.	☐	☐

8 In the text, find the words and expressions in *italics* which mean the same as the underlined words.

1 Don't talk to John! He's in a bad <u>temper</u>.

....

2 You can stay at my house <u>anytime you want</u>.

....

3 Cotton is a very cool <u>material</u>.

....

4 If you get ink on your clothes, it will <u>leave marks that you can't remove</u>.

....

5 Canoeists and skiers need clothes that <u>stay dry</u>.

....

Useful expressions

1 Match the questions (1–6) with the answers (a–f).

1 What do you want to do when you leave school? [b]

2 Why do you want to drop art next year? ☐

3 Are you going to go to drama school? ☐

4 Do you like French? ☐

5 Are you going to do chemistry or maths? ☐

6 What are you going to study at university? ☐

a Not really. I prefer science to languages.

b I'd like to train to be a paramedic.

c I want to do graphic design.

d Because I'd rather do media studies instead.

e Actually, I don't want to do either of those subjects.

f I don't think so. I'd rather be a musician than an actor.

2 Complete the dialogue with the missing sentences (a–f).

Daisy: Are you going to the fancy dress party on Saturday?

Neil: I'm not sure.

Daisy: Why not? Everyone else is going. It'll be fun.

Neil: I don't know. ....d..... I feel silly.

Daisy: You don't have to wear anything fancy. You could go as a Roman soldier or something like that.

Neil: Hmmm. [1]........... I don't want to get cold.

Daisy: I'm sure you won't! You'll be dancing and it'll be hot.

Neil: Actually, I hate dancing. [2]...........

Daisy: Oh, come on! I'll go to the fancy dress shop and help you choose a costume if you like.

Neil: Maybe. I'll think about it. So, what will you be wearing?

Daisy: I haven't decided yet. [3]...........

Neil: Are you going to hire one from the shop as well?

Daisy: Actually, I'm going to make one.

Neil: Won't that be a lot of work?

Daisy: Not really. [4]........... I could make one for you, too.

Neil: Thanks, but no thanks. [5]...........

Daisy: OK, OK. I won't mention it again!

a I think I'd rather wear something warmer!

b I don't want to go to the party, remember?

c I'd like to wear something really different.

d I don't really like dressing up and wearing costumes.

e Anyway, I prefer home-made costumes to hired costumes.

f In fact, I'd rather stay at home and watch TV than go out dancing.

3 Anna and Evie are in a clothes shop. Choose the correct options (a–c).

Anna: Look at these hooded tops! They're really nice.

Evie: Yes, they are, but I [1]........... tops without a hood.

Anna: Oh! I like these skirts.

Evie: Me too. But don't you think they're too short? I think I [2]........... wear something a bit longer.

Anna: You're right. What about this dress?

Evie: Ugh! It's awful! I don't [3]........... the pattern and I hate pastel pink!

Anna: OK, OK. Calm down!

Evie: Actually, I [4]........... to look in a different shop.

Anna: Sure. Where do you suggest?

Evie: Well, I [5]........... shorts and T-shirts to skirts and dresses. So why don't we go to the big sports shop on the high street?

Anna: Good idea! They have some really nice stuff there. And I [6]........... buy some new trainers as well.

1 **a** 'd rather   **b** prefer   **c** don't like

2 **a** want   **b** 'd rather   **c** 'd like

3 **a** like   **b** want   **c** prefer

4 **a** 'd like   **b** 'd rather   **c** like

5 **a** 'd rather   **b** prefer   **c** want

6 **a** prefer   **b** 'd rather   **c** want to

4 Complete the dialogue with the words in the box.

like	prefer	rather	than	~~to~~	to	want

David: I'm going to put my name down to do Sports Relief next month.

Jana: That's a good idea! I'd like *to* do something as well.

David: Well, the school are doing a sponsored run to raise money.

Jana: I'm not very good at athletics. I'd [1].......... play tennis [2].......... go running.

David: What about badminton? The leisure centre are organising a 24-hour tournament.

Jana: That sounds fun! Why don't you do it with me?

David: I [3].......... team sports [4].......... racket sports. In fact, I'd [5].......... to play in the three-legged football match at school. It's teachers versus students!

Jana: I definitely [6].......... to see that!

David: OK, but you'll have to sponsor me first!

Pronunciation: words with /s/ and /z/ sounds

5 🔊 *4.2* Listen and write the words in the box in the correct column in the table.

basketball business busy design disappear dress fossil hypnosis museum pleased presentation sponsor thousand used (*past simple*) used to

/s/	/z/

6 🔊 *4.3* Practise saying these sentences. Then listen and repeat.

1 I'm playing in a sponsored basketball match.

2 I'm giving a business presentation tomorrow.

3 He's designed thousands of dresses.

4 She looks after fossils in the museum.

5 People used to send messages by telegraph.

Writing: arrangements

7 Read the emails and answer the questions.

1 What are Jana and Daisy doing on Saturday?

2 Where is it going to take place?

3 Who is organising the event?

8 Read the emails again and circle the correct options (1–6).

Hi Jana,
I've just seen your name on the list for the sponsored badminton tournament on Saturday. I'll be taking part in the morning, but I don't know exactly when yet. I'll phone the coach [1] *until / when* I get home. If you're playing at the same time as me, you could come round to my house first and we can go together. I only live five minutes' walk from the leisure centre. I'll send you another email [2] *when / by the time* I find out what time we're playing.
Daisy

Hi Daisy,
I'm playing in the morning too. I phoned the leisure centre this afternoon to check what time, but the receptionist didn't have the list. She won't know [3] *until / when* the badminton coach arrives later this evening because the coach has organised all the matches. She's going to phone me back [4] *by the time / as soon as* she can. Anyway, [5] *until / by the time* you get home, I'll probably know when we're playing. I'll send you a message later this evening [6] *by the time / as soon as* I know more.
Jana

9 Complete the sentences with information from the emails in Exercise 8.

1 Jana and Daisy don't know exactly when
....

2 Daisy will phone the organiser as soon as
....

3 Daisy won't send Jana another email until
....

4 The coach will give the receptionist the list when she ....

5 By the time ....,
Jana will have the information they need.

6 Jana will send a text message when ....
....

10 Jana has spoken to the receptionist and has all the details. Write Jana's message to Daisy to confirm the times and arrange to meet. Make sure you use expressions such as *as soon as, by the time, when* and *until*.

Reading

1 **Read the text and choose the correct option (a–c).**

> My passion for making furniture started when I was young. My grandfather was a skilled carpenter and he taught me everything I know. After university, I got a job as a manager in a furniture store, but I continued to work on my own designs in my spare time. I design mainly tables and chairs. I don't use a computer because I'd rather use paper and pencils. I make the furniture in my workshop, which is in the garage. I spend most of my weekends in there. This year, I'm going to try and sell my work at a craft fair.

The text is about:

a the writer's job.

b the writer's plans.

c the writer's hobby.

2 **Read the text and choose the correct option (a–c).**

> During the 1980s, the film industry produced lots of blockbusters. Big hits included horror movies such as *The Terminator*, *Robocop* and *Alien*, as well as teen movies like *Dirty Dancing* and *The Breakfast Club*. However, there were also plenty of flops! Some of the worst films made were bad comedies and sci-fi movies like *Flash Gordon* and *Ishtar* and many more. However, the latest news is that Hollywood is planning to remake a number of '80s box office hits. The first to reach our screens will be *The Karate Kid*, *Nightmare on Elm Street* and *Predator*.

The text is about:

a popular movies.

b films of the 1980s.

c new Hollywood films.

3 **Read the text and choose the correct option (a–c).**

> Hi Auntie Jen,
>
> I ¹.......... a sponsored run for Sports Relief next Saturday. We ².......... raise lots of money for charity. We'll be running three miles and some people will be wearing fancy dress. Obviously, I ³.......... wearing a silly costume – just my shorts and a T-shirt. Anyway, I think it will be great ⁴..........!
>
> So, will you and Uncle Sam sponsor me? ⁵.......... really like you to come and watch as well. The run starts at 11 a.m. in the town centre and finishes at the school. I'll probably finish in less ⁶.......... an hour. I'll send you a sponsor form later.
>
> Love,
>
> David

1	**a** 'm doing	**b** will do	**c** do
2	**a** want	**b** want to	**c** like
3	**a** 'll be	**b** 'd like to	**c** won't be
4	**a** funny	**b** fun	**c** time
5	**a** I'll	**b** I'd	**c** I
6	**a** than	**b** that	**c** of

Word list Unit 4

accountant (n)	....		passionate (adj)	....
affect	....		pattern (n)	....
ankle (n)	....		physiotherapist (n)	....
bead (n)	....		pitch (n)	....
carpenter (n)	....		placement (n)	....
chef (n)	....		postal worker (n)	....
coach (n)	....		prediction (n)	....
court (n)	....		referee (n)	....
craft fair (n)	....		remake (v)	....
demand (n)	....		resemble (v)	....
denim (n)	....		round-neck (adj)	....
design (n & v)	....		skin-tight (adj)	....
electrician (n)	....		sleeve (n)	....
engineer (n)	....		slope (n)	....
equally (adv)	....		spare time (n)	....
flared (adj)	....		spectator (n)	....
flowered (adj)	....		spotted (adj)	....
footwear (n)	....		spray can (n)	....
force (n)	....		stadium (n)	....
garment (n)	....		stain (v)	....
haven't got a clue (phr)	....		striped (adj)	....
hooded (adj)	....		tight (adj)	....
ingredient (n)	....		tough (adj)	....
injury (n)	....		tournament (n)	....
law of motion (n phr)	....		track (n)	....
loose (adj)	....		trainer (n)	....
mood (n)	....		umpire (n)	....
nanoparticle (n)	....		waterproof (adj)	....
paramedic (n)	....		wild boar (n)	....
			workshop (n)	....

Grammar Practice Unit 4

future plans and arrangements

When we talk about future plans and arrangements, we can use the **future simple** (*will*), *going to*, the **present continuous** or the **present simple**. Each of these shows something slightly different about the plans/arrangements.

- *Will* is used to talk about decisions we make at the moment of speaking, usually about the near future.
  It's hot in here – I'll open the window.

- *going to* is used to talk about **plans** for the near future, but **without definite arrangements**.
  I'm going to save up all my pocket money so I can buy a new bike.
  We also use *going to* for **ambitions**.
  I'm going to go to university when I leave school.

- the **present continuous** is used to talk about **definite arrangements** for the near future; we usually know and mention the specific day/ date, time and place.
  I'm travelling to Edinburgh tomorrow on the Intercity train.

- the **present simple** is used to talk about **timetabled** arrangements.
  The play starts at 8.15, so I'll meet you in the foyer of the theatre at eight o'clock.

1 Circle the correct option.

It's cold today, so I think (I'll wear) / I'm wearing a coat.

1 Let's go to the match today. It *starts / will start* at three o'clock.

2 I'*m going / I'll go* for a haircut after school – I've already made an appointment.

3 I need a break – I'*ll finish / finish* my homework later.

4 Dad'*s leaving / will leave* for Paris at 8.30 on Friday.

5 Guy *will / is going to* buy Tess a CD for her birthday.

2 Complete the sentences with the future simple, *going to*, present continuous or present simple form of the verbs in brackets.

I need some new clothes, so I'm going to go (go) shopping later.

1 It's hot in here, isn't it? I .... (open) the window.

2 Hurry up – my favourite TV programme .... (start) in five minutes.

3 Tina wants to lose weight, so she .... (go) on a diet.

4 Have you decided what you .... (do) when you leave school?

5 The band .... (play) a concert in Dublin on 14 July.

6 Are you hungry? I .... (make) you an omelette.

3 Write sentences. Use the future simple, going to or present continuous form of the verbs.

You / get / a holiday job / this summer?

Are you going to get a holiday job this summer?

1 Mike / do / his French exam / on Thursday morning.

....

2 My mobile has run out of battery – I / charge / it / after school.

....

3 The football team / start / training / early / this year.

....

4 The class / visit / the science museum / next Wednesday.

....

5 I / paint / my bedroom a blue-grey colour.

....

predictions

- We can use *will*, *may* and *might* for predictions about the future, based on what we think, believe or hope.
  One day scientists will probably discover how to stop us getting old.

- We can use *going to* for predictions about the future, based on some evidence in the present.
  The sky is dark. There's going to be a storm.

Will, *may* and *might* have the same form for all subjects (*I, you, he,* etc). The main verb after these modals is in the **bare infinitive**.

The negative of *will* is **won't** (*will not*) and it is the same for all subjects. The negative of *may* and *might* is **may not** and **might not**, and these are also the same for all subjects.

Using *may* instead of *will* often suggests we are not so sure about our prediction, and *might* usually suggests we are even less sure. We often use these modals after *I think, I'm sure,* etc, and/ or with words such as *probably, perhaps, certainly,* etc, to show more clearly how sure we are about our prediction.

I'm sure I will find an interesting career when I leave school.

I think I may work in the world of finance.

Perhaps I might even become an accountant.

4 Complete the sentences with the future simple or *going to* form of the verbs in brackets.

The weather forecast said that it's *going to get* (get) very cold tonight.

1 I think there's a good chance that we .... (win) the match on Saturday.

2 Statistics show that the problem of global warming .... (continue) for some time.

3 Perhaps researchers .... (find) a cure for this disease soon.

4 Jo wants to go to the concert, but I don't think she .... (manage) to get tickets.

5 The school play .... (be) a disaster – none of the actors know their lines.

other uses of *will*

Will is also used for:

- offers
  I'll carry that bag for you.
- promises
  I'll never do that again, I promise!
- warnings
  If you do that again, I'll tell Mum!
- requests
  Will you help me with my homework?
- statements of fact about the future
  Mr Wilson will be 83 next week.

future continuous

The **future continuous** is used for actions that (we expect or predict) will be in progress at a specific time in the future.

At this time tomorrow, I'll be having a French lesson.

We form the future continuous with *will/won't* + *be* + *-ing*. It has the same form for all subjects (*I, he, we,* etc.).

We form questions in the future continuous by putting *will* before the subject and then *be*, followed by the *-ing* form of the main verb.

5 Complete the sentences with the future continuous form of the verbs in brackets.

In a few weeks' time, I'*ll be swimming* (swim) in the Caribbean.

1 Let's meet at eleven o'clock. I .... (wait) at the station.

2 I .... (not live) with my parents when I'm 25.

3 At the end of June, I .... (camp) in Wales.

4 By the time he's thirty, Steve .... (earn) lots of money.

5 In ten years' time, everyone .... (wear) completely different fashions.

6 Write sentences. Use the future continuous form of the verbs.

What / you / do / at lunchtime on Saturday?
What will you be doing at lunchtime on Saturday?

1 At this time tomorrow evening, / I / baby-sit / for the people next door.
....

2 You / travel / around Europe / during your gap year?
....

3 In two years from now, I / drive / my own car.
....

4 You can borrow my camera for your school trip – I / not use / it.
....

5 Karen / work / part-time in December?
....

time expressions used for the future

Time expressions such as *after, as soon as, before, by the time, when, while* and *until* can be used to talk about the future, but they are not followed by *will*. Instead, they are followed by a **present tense** (usually the present simple).

- *after, before* – used to show a sequence of actions/events
  I'll do my homework after I have dinner.
- *as soon as* – emphasises 'immediately after this'
  I'll send you an email as soon as I get home.
- *by the time* – means 'at some time before this'
  It'll be dark by the time we arrive.
- *when* – means 'at this time'
  Let me know when you decide what you're going to do.
- *while* – used for two things happening at the same time; mainly used with continuous tenses
  I'll be studying while my friends are having fun.
- *until* – shows that something will happen after a specific time but not before
  Please remain seated until the aircraft comes to a complete stop.

7 Circle the correct option.

I'll let you know as soon as I (*hear*)/ '*ll hear* any news.

1 You can't watch TV *by the time / until* you finish your homework.

2 *I call / I'll call* my parents when we arrive at the coach station.

3 Check your work for mistakes before you *hand / 'll hand* it in.

4 Let's go for a walk *when / while* the rain stops.

5 Don't forget to lock the front door *after / before* you go to bed.

6 I'll sort out my files when I'*ll have / have* some free time.

Review Units 3 and 4

Grammar review: *verb + -ing* and *to + infinitive*

1 Complete the sentences with the correct verb form: *-ing* or *to + infinitive*.

1 Everyone has agreed .... (meet) at the park.

2 Has Rachel finished .... (dry) her hair yet?

3 Sean is really bad at .... (swim).

4 We have decided .... (go) skiing this winter.

5 .... (learn) English is easy.

6 Martina isn't interested in .... (learn) to play tennis.

7 It's impossible .... (understand) this text. It's too complicated.

8 I can't imagine .... (live) in another country.

9 Marco Polo is famous for .... (discover) the Americas.

10 I don't recommend .... (eat) at that restaurant. It's terrible!

11 I enjoyed .... (talk) to Rosie at the party.

12 What do you hope .... (find out) from the expedition?

13 Let's go inside. It's starting .... (rain).

14 On our trek, we didn't stop .... (walk) until we reached camp.

15 At 3 o'clock every afternoon, the workers stop .... (have) a tea break.

1 mark per item: ...... / 15 marks

Past tenses

2 Complete the sentences with the past simple or past perfect form of the verbs.

1 We .... (leave) school early yesterday because the snow .... (start) to settle on the ground.

2 After I .... (say) goodbye to my friends, I .... (catch) the bus home.

3 Mum .... (go) shopping so there .... (be) nobody in.

4 I .... (have to) wait outside because I .... (forget) my key.

5 By the time Mum .... (arrive) home, I .... (be) freezing cold!

1 mark per item: ...... / 10 marks

3 How many of the options (a, b or c) can be used to complete the sentences? Circle the options which are correct.

1 When I was a child, I .... camping.
   a used to love   **b** loved   **c** had loved

2 My little sister .... vegetables.
   a didn't eat   **b** didn't use to eat   **c** hadn't eaten

3 Last year we .... a canal boat in France for two weeks.
   a had hired   **b** used to hire   **c** hired

4 It was a lovely day, so we all .... to swim in the river.
   a decided   **b** used to decide   **c** had decided

5 .... have mobile phones in the '80s?
   a Did they   **b** Did they use to   **c** Used they to

2 marks per item: ...... / 10 marks

4 Complete the text with the words in the box.

bought   developed   had   had bought   had thought
had used   saw   used to   was   went

I ¹..................... a teenager in the '90s and I remember the day when I first ²..................... a computer with a Windows operating system. I thought it was amazing! Up until then, I ³..................... that computers were both boring and annoying. They ⁴..................... big, heavy monitors with black-and-white screens and they always ⁵..................... go wrong. But after the arrival of Windows, computer technology ⁶..................... really quickly. My dad ⁷..................... me a PC a few years later, when I ⁸..................... to university. Up until then, I ⁹..................... a pen and paper to do all my schoolwork. By the end of the '90s, many people ¹⁰..................... computers for their homes.

1 mark per item: ...... /10 marks

Future tenses

5 Circle the correct future form of the verb.

1 What will *you do / you be doing* when you leave school?

2 By the time Sam gets up, I *will be sitting / am going to sit* on the plane to Paris.

3 In two months from now, Sarah and Alex will *be living / live* in Canada.

4 Biddeford United will probably *lose / be losing* the match next Saturday.

5 By 2020, every student in Britain *will be using / is using* a laptop computer in the classroom.

1 mark per item: ...... / 5 marks

Vocabulary review: Archaeology

6 Match the words in the box with the definitions.

> archaeologist artefact fossil
> fragment palaeontologist remains

1 a person who studies objects from the past
....

2 an ancient plant or animal contained in rock
....

3 a tiny piece of a broken object ....

4 an ancient object made by a person ....

5 what is left of an ancient building or object
....

6 a person who studies life forms from prehistoric times ....

1 mark per item: ...... / 6 marks

Cooking

7 Complete the sentences with the words in the box and the correct option.

> apples beef bread curry eggs

1 A typical British Sunday dinner includes *roast / baked* .... and potatoes.

2 My grandmother *bakes / slices* her own .... in the oven.

3 To make an Indian ...., you start by *chopping / grilling* vegetables into pieces.

4 My dad is brilliant at *peeling / slicing* .... – the skin comes off in one long piece.

5 *Boiling / Grilling* .... is easy. You just have to make sure the water is covering them.

2 marks per item: ...... / 10 marks

American and British English

8 Circle the correct option to complete the emails.

Hi Luke,
How are things in the UK? I just got back from the [1] *diner / restaurant* where we went to eat lunch. I had a large steak and [2] *chips / fries*. It was delicious! Next week is Thanksgiving [3] *holiday / vacation* and we're going skiing. I need some new ski [4] *pants / trousers*, so we're going to the sports [5] *shop / store* downtown. My brother is calling me for a game of basketball, so I've got to go.
Ben

Hi Ben,
You must have a really big [6] *yard / garden* if you can play basketball there! We live in a [7] *flat / apartment* in London, so we have to go to the park. It was my birthday last week and I got a new [8] *cell phone / mobile*. As I was leaving the house, the [9] *mailman / postman* handed me a huge pile of envelopes. I opened them at [10] *break time / recess* with my friends. Hope you enjoy your skiing trip!
Luke

1 mark per item: ...... / 10 marks

Communicate

9 Complete the questions.

1 A: .... is it from school to your house?
B: About half a mile.

2 A: .... does it take to make an omelette?
B: About ten minutes.

3 A: .... do you spend on bus fares?
B: Five pounds a week.

4 A: .... ago did you pass your driving test?
B: Two months ago.

5 A: .... does it cost to go to the theatre?
B: I'm not sure, but I think it's quite expensive.

6 A: .... do you go to the gym?
B: Twice a week.

7 A: .... students are there in your class?
B: Twenty-five.

2 marks per item: ...... / 14 marks

10 Complete the dialogues with the words in the box.

> do you don't want How much I'd like
> prefer rather than What time Where

1

A: [1]...................... does the leisure centre close?

B: At seven. Why?

A: [2]...................... like to go swimming this afternoon.

B: I'll come with you. But I'd rather work out in the gym [3]...................... go for a swim.

2

A: I've booked our tickets for the gymnastics event. So, [4]...................... want to take the bus to London or the train?

B: I'd [5]...................... to go by train. It's more comfortable.

A: I agree, but it's more expensive. I'd [6]...................... spend my money on something else.

B: Yes, well, I [7]...................... to get travel sick, so I'm not going on the bus!

3

A: [8]...................... did you learn to dance?

B: I go to dance classes in town. Would you [9]...................... to come with me?

A: I'd love to. [10]...................... does it cost?

1 mark per item: ...... / 10 marks

Total: ...... / 100 marks

5A World wonders

Vocabulary: materials

1 Read the clues and complete the crossword puzzle.

Across

2 It is used to make windows.

4 It comes from an animal and we make jumpers from it.

5 It is made from trees. Nowadays, it is often recycled.

8 Trees are cut down to produce this material which is used to make many things including furniture, buildings and household objects.

9 Clothes, bedclothes and sofa covers are made from this. Cotton, silk and denim are all examples of it.

10 Many English houses are built from this man-made material. It is often red.

11 This is the best material for making shoes and handbags.

Down

1 Most knives, forks and spoons are made of this hard material.

3 Many old buildings, such as castles and churches, are made of this. Sculptors also use it to make statues.

5 A material which is produced using chemical processes. As it can be shaped into different forms and take different colours it is used to make many things including children's toys.

6 It comes from a special type of tree and is used to make car tyres.

7 This is a man-made material which is very strong and solid. It is used to build houses, bridges and some roads.

2 Complete the sentences with *as*, *for* or *to*.

1 The temples at Chichén Itzá were used .... making sacrifices.

2 The Emperor Shah Jahan built the Taj Mahal .... a monument to his wife.

3 Huge stones from Wales were used .... build Stonehenge.

4 The Tower of London used to be used .... a prison.

5 I went to England last year .... improve my English.

6 Did you visit Dublin .... business or pleasure?

Grammar: passive

3 Complete the sentences with the correct passive form of the verb in brackets.

1 The original 'Seven Wonders of the World' list .... during the Middle Ages. (write)

2 The Great Pyramid at Giza .... at the top of the original list. (place)

3 The Great Pyramid .... on any new 'Seven Wonders' lists since 2007. (not included)

4 Many Egyptians died while the pyramid .... (build)

5 New 'Seven Wonders' lists .... all the time. (create)

6 Many different sites .... as the Eighth Wonder of the world. (nominate)

4 Rewrite each active sentence in the passive.

More than three million people visit Yellowstone National Park in the USA every year.

Yellowstone National Park in the USA is visited by more than three million people every year.

1 Many famous people have visited the Salt Mines.

....
....

2 Until recently, humidity was eroding the salt sculptures.

....
....

3 UNESCO listed Malbork Castle as a World Heritage site in 1997.

....
....

4 In 1945, fighting destroyed about half of Malbork Castle.

....
....

5 They are still restoring parts of the castle.

....
....

6 Nobody has rebuilt the main cathedral yet.

....
....

Vocabulary: size and shape

5 Circle the correct option.

1 Rugby is played with a(n) *oval* / *round* ball.

2 The O2 Arena in London is *microscopic* / *immense*. It holds up to 23,000 people.

3 Most buildings have *rectangular* / *triangular* windows.

4 I've just eaten a *huge* / *tiny* meal and now I don't feel well!

5 Sea horses are *little* / *massive* sea creatures.

6 Football fields are usually *square* / *rectangular* in shape.

Working with words: adjective order

6 Complete the descriptions (1–6) opposite using adjectives from the box.

ancient	black	broken	Egyptian	expensive
grey	huge	leather	shiny	small	stone
white	wooden

1 a(n) ...., ... bag

2 a(n) ...., ... rabbit and a big, ... rabbit

3 a(n) ...., ... mummy

4 a(n) ...., ... chair

5 a(n) ...., ... London taxi

6 a(n) ...., ... sculpture

7 Put the words in the correct order to make sentences.

1 the / made / pots / beautiful / ancient Greeks / ceramic

The ....

2 huge / bought / wooden / a / table / round / we

We ....

3 actress / wore / a / long / dress / red / to / the / lovely / the / ceremony

The ....

4 grandmother / silk / I / new / scarf / her / gave / Chinese / my / a / birthday / for

I ....

5 a / modern / in / let's / tonight / stay / hotel / American / nice

Let's ....

6 there / many / too / ugly /concrete / are / city / grey / buildings / my / in

There ....

Reading

1 Read Becky's blog about the Fairtrade Foundation. Tick (✓) the products she mentions.

☐ balls ☐ baskets ☐ chocolate ☐ clothing
☐ coffee ☐ fruit ☐ jewellery ☐ pottery
☐ rice ☐ scarves ☐ soap ☐ tea

2 Read the text again. Choose the best title (a, b or c).

a What is Fairtrade?
b My trip to a Fairtrade community
c My week learning about Fairtrade

Last month, I did a week's work experience at the Fairtrade Foundation in London. I chose this organisation because we use such a lot of foreign products at home, and I wanted to find out about where they come from and who they are produced by. For example, a lot of our food comes from countries in South America and Africa. As the farmers in these countries don't have much economic power, they can't demand high prices. Did you know that a farmer sometimes only gets one penny of the 30 pence I pay for a banana?

The Fairtrade Foundation was started in 1992 to help farmers abroad get better and fairer prices for their products. It ensures farmers receive a fair price for their coffee, for example, one that does not fall below what it costs to produce. They also earn an extra amount, the Fairtrade premium, to decide for themselves how to invest in their communities and businesses. The first Fairtrade product here in the UK was Green & Black's Maya Gold chocolate. Nowadays, there are about 3,000 products on sale in UK shops, including clothing, other types of food and drink, sports balls and beauty products.

The Fairtrade Foundation helps developing world communities to grow and gives people the opportunity to improve their lives in many ways. For example, with the extra money they make, parents can afford to send their children to school for the first time. I especially liked the way Fairtrade is improving women's lives in many communities. In Burkina Faso the women produce shea butter, which is sold in Europe and is used in cooking and in soaps and moisturisers. The money they earn is important to the local economy and as a result, women are treated better and have more influence within their communities.

By the end of the week, it was clear to me how important Fairtrade is – and how easy it is to support. All you have to do is look for the Fairtrade label on goods in shops and supermarkets. As well as buying Fairtrade goods yourself, you can encourage your family and friends to start doing the same. You can even get your school to buy Fairtrade sports balls and school uniforms made from Fairtrade cotton. That's what I'm going to do this term! And there is a lot of information about organising a campaign in your school on the Fairtrade website.

Becky, North Devon, UK

3 Read the text again. Are the sentences true or false?

	T	F
1 A lot of our food is produced abroad.	☐	☐
2 Farmers in poor countries are paid about 30 pence a day.	☐	☐
3 The Fairtrade Foundation was set up by British farmers.	☐	☐
4 Fairtrade farmers are involved in deciding how to invest their money.	☐	☐
5 Fairtrade products have been sold in Britain for more than 30 years.	☐	☐
6 Because of Fairtrade, women are becoming more powerful because they are able to bring money into the community.	☐	☐
7 At Becky's school, all students wear uniforms made with Fairtrade cotton.	☐	☐

Grammar: passive with modal verbs

4 Complete the sentences with the passive form of the verb.

1 Fairtrade products can .... in many shops. (buy)

2 Prices must .... by the farmer and the buyer. (agree)

3 Thanks to Fairtrade, people's lives can .... in many ways. (improve)

4 More children will .... an education. (give)

5 Fairtrade labels must .... clearly on each Fairtrade product. (show)

6 The new World Shop will .... by the mayor. (open)

Listening

5 **5.1** Listen to Becky talking to her friend Josh about how to recognise Fair Trade products in the shops. How many different Fair Trade labels does she talk about?

a one **b** two **c** three

6 **Listen again and complete the notes. Write one word in each gap.**

   1 The FAIRTRADE Mark is not difficult to
      ....

   2 The FAIRTRADE Mark on stickers is often stuck onto the skin of fresh fruit like .... and ....

   3 For goods such as coffee, rice or chocolate, you will find the FAIRTRADE Mark on the
      ....

   4 You can usually buy Fair Trade food in
      ....

   5 World Shops sell lots of different ....

   6 World Shops are found in most .... countries.

   7 The European Fair Trade Association label just uses the letters EFTA written in ....

7 **Complete the text with the active or passive form of the verbs in brackets.**

Working with words: verb + preposition

8 **Circle the correct option for each sentence.**

   1 My sister works *for* / *as* a clothing company.

   2 Did you compete *on* / *in* last week's race?

   3 In this part of the factory, the cocoa beans are made *from* / *into* a chocolate paste.

   4 Do you believe *on* / *in* ghosts?

   5 Can you think *to* / *of* a better idea?

   6 Poor farmers rely *on* / *in* Fair Trade to give them a fair price.

   7 The archaeologists were looking *on* / *for* Roman artefacts.

   8 Can you translate this text *into* / *for* English for me?

A very special vegetable

Have you ever eaten Mexican food? Do you know what chilli peppers are? Recently, these small, hot peppers [1]..................... (become) popular with cooks all over the world. Nowadays, they can [2]..................... (eat) in restaurants all over the world. However, chilli peppers [3]..................... (grow) in South America for more than 9,000 years. Christopher Columbus [4]..................... (see) the plants in 1492 and he [5]..................... (take) some back to Europe with him. Later, chillis [6]..................... (bring) into Africa and Asia by other traders.

Chilli peppers are full of vitamins and are very good for you. But did you know that chilli peppers are also a natural painkiller? Chillies [7]..................... (use) by the ancient Maya people to treat toothache, and the aztecs [8]..................... (put) chillies on their bodies to treat aches and pains. Today's scientists [9]..................... (discover) that the chemical in chilli peppers, called capsaicin, can kill pain. In fact, two capsaicin products [10]..................... (already / develop): a capsaicin cream and a painkiller for mouth pain. In the near future, these products [11]..................... (probably / sell) in most high street chemists.

Useful expressions

1 Match the questions (1–6) with the answers (a–f).

1 Why are you wearing so much make-up? ☐
2 What do you want to buy a motorbike for? ☐
3 What do you need all that paint for? ☐
4 Why are you saving all those stamps? ☐
5 What's that huge piece of cardboard for? ☐
6 Why did Sean stay up all night? ☐

a So that I can be more independent.
b It's for my art project.
c To finish his science project.
d Because I'm going to a party.
e To decorate my bedroom.
f Because I want to start a collection.

2 Adam and Julie are at a second-hand market. Complete the gaps (1–7) with the options (a–g).

Adam: How much are these old records?
Woman: They're fifty pence each.
Adam: Great. I'll take the whole box!
Julie: ¹..........
Adam: ²..........

Julie: Look at this big, straw hat. It's fantastic! I'm going to buy it!
Adam: Why? You never wear hats! ³..........
Julie: ⁴..........
Adam: I suppose that makes sense. It suits you too.

Adam: Look at this beautiful wooden toy. I bought it for Emma.
Julie: ⁵.......... She's too old for children's toys.
Adam: OK ... Oh, look! I like that pair of dark sunglasses.

Julie: ⁶.......... You've got some already.
Adam: ⁷..........

a What did you get that for?
b To keep the sun off my face on the beach.
c What do you need it for?
d Why do you want them?
e They're for my grandfather's birthday. He collects them.
f So that I can look cool, of course!
g What do you want to buy so many for?

3 Complete the dialogue with the words in the box.

because	for	so	to (×2)	what	why (×2)

Adam: Mum, look what I found in the attic! What is it? Can I take it to Julie's garage sale?

Mum: Let me see. Oh yes, it's a perfume bottle and it belonged to your great-great-grandmother.

Adam: ¹.................... did she use it for?

Mum: ².................... put perfume in, of course.

Adam: But when you buy perfume, it's already in a bottle. ³.................... did she want to put it into another one?

Mum: ⁴.................... that she could take some perfume with her when she went out.

Adam: It's quite heavy. ⁵.................... did she want a silver bottle?

Mum: ⁶.................... be fashionable. Look how pretty it is! In those days, women loved pretty boxes and bottles. And men used to buy them as gifts. And no, of course you can't take it to the garage sale!

Adam: Why not? What do you want to keep it ⁷....................?

Mum: ⁸.................... it's very special to me. Besides, it's made of solid silver and it's probably worth a lot of money.

Pronunciation: the letter *o* and the vowel sounds /əʊ/ and /ʌ/

4 🔊 **5.2** Say the pairs of words aloud and circle the word in each pair which contains the /əʊ/ sound. Then listen and check your answers.

1	above	erode	**4**	phone	some
2	clothes	other	**5**	wonder	local
3	done	stone	**6**	lovely	oval

Writing: a description of an object

5 **Read about a present that changed Mandy's life. Answer the questions.**

1 What was the present?
2 What was it like?
3 How did the present change Mandy's life?

When I was ten years old, my aunt gave me a set of three balls for my birthday. They were made of a soft, colourful fabric and each one fitted perfectly in my small hand. The other nice thing about them was that each contained a small bell which rang when the balls moved. The balls were for juggling with. As I don't have any brothers or sisters they were an especially good present for me because I could play with them on my own. After a while, I became really good at juggling and I decided that I wanted to join a juggling club. Since there wasn't a club in my town, I had to travel to the nearest big city, but it was well worth it! I've learned all sorts of other circus skills, including riding a unicycle and walking on stilts. Nowadays, I perform with the club at festivals and we all have a fantastic time. Those three little juggling balls really changed my life.

6 **Rewrite the second sentence so that it means the same as the first sentence. Use *as*, *because*, *since* or *so*. There may be more than one possible answer.**

1 I didn't have any brothers or sisters so I used to play a lot on my own.
I used to play ....
....

2 The balls were a great present because I didn't need anyone to do juggling with.
I didn't need ....
....

3 I wanted to join a club because I was becoming quite good at juggling.
....
...., I wanted to join a club.

4 Since there wasn't a club in my town, I had to travel to the nearest big city.
There wasn't a club ....
....

5 I learned so many things, so the journey to the club was worth it.
The journey ....
....

6 I often perform at festivals as I'm really good at juggling now.
....
...................................., I often perform at festivals.

7 **Think about an object (or objects) which changed your life. Read the questions below and make notes.**

When did you get the object?
....
What did it look like?
....
How did it feel?
....
What was special about it?
....
What did you do with it?
....
How did it make a difference to your life?
....

8 **Write your description. Use Mandy's description to help you. Remember to include *as*, *because*, *since* or *so*.**

Reading

1 Read the text. Are the sentences true or false?

> The Hanging Gardens of Babylon were one of the original Seven Wonders of the Ancient World. They were built in 600 BC by King Nebuchadnezzar II to make his wife happy because she missed the green vegetation and mountains of her homeland in Persia. The gardens were built high above the ground on huge terraces. They were supported by massive stone columns and water from the river was pumped to the top to water the gardens. The gardens were destroyed by earthquakes around 200BC. However, some experts believe that the gardens never existed at all.

		T	F
1	King Nebuchadnezzar built the Hanging Gardens to please his wife.	☐	☐
2	The gardens were built on the side of a mountain.	☐	☐
3	Water was carried every day from the river to water the gardens.	☐	☐
4	The gardens were destroyed in a natural disaster four hundred years after they were built.	☐	☐

Listening

2 🔘 5.3 Listen to the phone messages (1–3) and complete the missing information.

1
```
Message for: ¹......................
Message from: Lucy
Message: staying at a friend's
house for ²..................... .
Please pick me up at about
³..................... .
```

2
Message for: *Stacey*
Message from: *The leisure centre*
Message: They need a ¹..................... for the basketball team.
Call ²..................... ASAP.
Contact number: ³..................... .

3
Message for: ¹.....................
Message from: the bookshop
Message: ²..................... has arrived.
You can pick it up anytime between ³..................... and ⁴..................... .

Word list / Unit 5

artificial (adj)	....	moisturiser (n)	....
artificially (adv)	....	natural resource (n)	....
attic (n)	....	nugget (n)	....
bedclothes (n pl)	....	nursing (n)	....
boom town (n)	....	opportunity (n)	....
brick (n)	....	oval (adj)	....
capsaicin (n)	....	painkiller (n)	....
commemorate (v)	....	population (n)	....
compound (n)	....	possession (n)	....
concrete (n)	....	promote (v)	....
contain (v)	....	pure (adj)	....
cure (v)	....	rectangular (adj)	....
dense (adj)	....	rectangular (adj)	....
dentistry (n)	....	(the) Redeemer (n)	....
digital (adj)	....	rely on (v)	....
digitally (adv)	....	rubber (n)	....
ensure (v)	....	shiny (adj)	....
erect (v)	....	skyscraper (n)	....
fabric (n)	....	solid (adj)	....
favour (n)	....	spectacular (adj)	....
feature (v)	....	spice (n)	....
gold rush (n)	....	square (adj)	....
humidity (n)	....	sticker (n)	....
identical (adj)	....	stilts (n pl)	....
immense (adj)	....	thread (n)	....
intricate (adj)	....	tiny (adj)	....
juggling (n)	....	trade route (n)	....
label (n)	....	triangular (adj)	....
limestone (n)	....	treasure (n)	....
marble (n)	....	treasured (adj)	....
massive (adj)	....	unicycle (n)	....
mayor (n)	....	vast (adj)	....
microscopic (adj)	....		

the passive: present simple, past simple, present continuous, past continuous, present perfect

In active voice, the subject of the sentence is the person or thing that does the action. When we use the **passive**, the subject is the person or thing that the action happens to.

In other words, the object of a sentence in active voice becomes the subject of the sentence in the passive. If we want to say who/what does the action (the agent) in the passive, we use **by**.

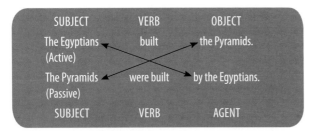

SUBJECT	VERB	OBJECT
The Egyptians (Active)	built	the Pyramids.
The Pyramids (Passive)	were built	by the Egyptians.
SUBJECT	VERB	AGENT

We use the passive when we want to emphasise the subject and/or the action itself. If it is not important or not clear who/what the agent is (e.g. *someone*, *they*, *people*), then we don't include it.

***They** discovered the well-preserved body of a baby mammoth.*
(Not: *The well-preserved body of a baby mammoth was discovered by them.*)

tenses in the passive

We form the passive with *be* + **the past participle** of the verb which is used in the active sentence. The tense of *be* is the same as the tense of the verb in the active sentence.

*People often **photograph** Stonehenge at sunrise.*
(present simple)
*Stonehenge **is** often **photographed** by people at sunrise.*

*A volcanic eruption **destroyed** the island.* (past simple)
*The island **was destroyed** by a volcanic eruption.*

*Contact with the outside world **is** slowly **changing** the local culture.* (present continuous)
*The local culture **is** slowly **being changed** by contact with the outside world.*

*They **were studying** the stars long before Galileo.*
(past continuous)
*The stars **were being studied** long before Galileo.*

*They **have uncovered** several Stone Age tools.*
(present perfect)
*Several Stone Age tools **have been uncovered**.*

1 **Rewrite the sentences in the passive.**

100,000 tourists a year visit the ancient site.
The ancient site is visited by 100,000 tourists a year.

1 They have restored some historic buildings in the old town.
....

2 They were repairing the monument when it collapsed.
....

3 Smog and acid rain are destroying the marble statues.
....

4 They made new discoveries at the site recently.
....

5 Ancient tools provide information about life in the past.
....

6 Roman senators assassinated Julius Caesar.
....

2 **Rewrite the sentences in the active or passive.**

It is not known for certain who the statues were carved by.
They don't know for certain who carved the statues.

1 They are researching a cure for the common cold.
....

2 The explosion destroyed dozens of houses.
....

3 Windows in the building have been broken by angry protesters.
....

4 A new plan was announced by the government yesterday.
....

5 Shelters give homeless people a place to sleep.
....

the negative form and questions in the passive

We form the negative by adding *n't* (*not*) to the first modal/auxiliary in the sentence – that is, *isn't/aren't* in the present simple/continuous, *wasn't/weren't* in the past simple/continuous and *hasn't/haven't* in the present perfect.

*Volcanic eruptions **aren't caused** by human activity.*
*The horse **wasn't being ridden** when it broke its leg.*
*A final decision **hasn't been reached** yet.*

We form questions in the passive by putting the first modal/auxiliary in the sentence – *Is/Are, Was/Were* or *Has/Have* – before the subject.

***Have** any steps **been taken** to improve the situation?*

We can also begin questions with question words such as *What, Why, Where, How,* etc.
***What** is climate change **caused by**?*

3 Rewrite the sentences as questions or negative sentences.

> The young Pharaoh was buried in the Valley of the Kings. (?)
>
> *Was the young Pharaoh buried in the Valley of the Kings?*

1 Evidence has been found to support this theory. (?)

....

2 Records of these events were written by people who saw them. (✗)

....

3 The archaeological finds were excavated carefully. (✗)

....

4 Important new discoveries are still being made today. (?)

....

the passive with modal verbs

If a sentence in active voice contains a modal such as *can/can't, must/mustn't* or *will/won't*, the modal is followed by the **bare infinitive**. In the same way, if a sentence in the passive contains one of these modals, the modal is followed by the bare infinitive of *be* and then the past participle of the main verb.

*We **must save** endangered species from extinction.*
*Endangered species **must be saved** from extinction.*

4 Rewrite the sentences in the passive.

> They will release the film in December.
>
> *The film will be released in December.*

1 You must store this medicine in the fridge.

....

2 You can't separate pure gold into different materials.

....

3 You can use gold for so many different things.

....

4 They may find new uses for gold in the future.

....

5 You mustn't lock the emergency exit doors.

....

causative form

We use **causative form** to talk about an action which the subject does not do themselves. That is, someone else does the action for them (e.g. cuts their hair, fixes their computer), but the subject has the result of the action (a new haircut, a computer that works properly, etc).

The causative form is ***have* + object + past participle** of the main verb. *Have* is used as a normal verb in any tense.
*I **have my hair cut** every month.* (The hairdresser cuts it.)
*They **had their house painted** last month.* (Painters painted it.)
*Sandra's **going to have her hair dyed**.* (The hairdresser is going to dye it.)
*Dad **has had his car repaired**.* (A mechanic has repaired it.)

As with the passive, we don't mention the agent (that is, the person who actually does the action) if it is obvious, not important or not clear.
She's having her teeth checked on Friday ~~by the dentist~~.

We can also use ***get* + object + past participle**, especially with tenses for the future, to emphasise that we will make arrangements for someone else to do something for us, or tell someone else to do it.

5 Rewrite the sentences in the causative form.

> Someone has installed solar panels on our roof.
>
> *We've had solar panels installed on our roof.*

1 The hairdresser has just cut Holly's hair.

....

2 My grandfather never wanted anyone to take his photo.

....

3 The optician tested my eyes a month ago.

....

4 Someone is servicing Mum's car tomorrow.

....

5 Someone is going to cut down the tree in our garden.

....

6A A literary mystery

Vocabulary: types of books

1 Read the book reviews (1–6) and match them with the covers (a–f).

1 Deirdre Pepper is one of my favourite [1]..................... book authors. Her recipes are simple yet delicious. Although written more than a decade ago, this book is still a bestseller and is certain to become a [2]..................... .

2 Sue Spence's writing is exciting and her plots are full of surprises. This latest [3]..................... is a murder [4]..................... set in Rome. It's a real page-turner and the identity of the murderer remains unknown right up until the last page.

3 Kathryn Epoch has done it again! Full of interesting detail and wonderful description, this [5]..................... novel, set in the time of Louis XIV, is a pleasure to read.

4 Feride Kerem's modern-day [6]..................... will interest teenage boys as well as girls. Halil, the hero of the story, is in love with the wrong girl. If his parents find out, there will be terrible consequences.

5 Poet Tom Keating lived a full and interesting life. After months of research and interviews with his family, Sally Hughes has written a brilliant [7]..................... about this fascinating man.

6 This is a [8]..................... story with a difference, as it contains both [9]..................... and an exciting, original plot. Inspector Smilie is investigating a series of art forgeries. However, he makes lots of mistakes and the consequences are often very funny!

2 Complete the reviews in Exercise 1 with the words in the box. There is one extra word.

autobiography biography classic cookery detective
historical humour mystery romance thriller

Vocabulary: art and books

3 Circle the correct option.

1 Before cameras were invented, rich people had their *portraits / still life* painted.

2 You need high-quality paper and pencils to do a good *drawing / painting*.

3 Picasso is famous for his *sculptures / abstract works of art*.

4 Shakespeare's *Othello* is a *play / poetry* about jealousy and love.

5 *Landscape / Watercolour* paint is easy to use because it dries quickly.

6 You shouldn't mix *oil / watercolour* paints with water.

7 The *fiction / non-fiction* section in our library has a lot of books about local history.

4 Two people are looking round an art gallery in Scotland. Complete the dialogue with words from Exercise 3. Use plural forms where necessary.

A: I don't really like this picture. It's too [1]..................... for me. I mean, what's it supposed to be, exactly?

B: I'm not sure, but I think it's some kind of [2]..................... . I think the shapes represent a table with fruit on it. I think the artist must have used a knife to apply the [3]..................... paint.

A: You're right. It's certainly very thick and shiny. It's my favourite [4]..................... so far. Hey, look at that huge picture of some mountains over there, in the next room.

B: I think it's Ben Nevis. It's enormous, isn't it? That must be the room with all the [5]..................... in. Shall we go and have a look?

A: OK, but I really want to go and see the [6]..................... of the old Scottish kings and queens after that.

Working with words: phrasal verbs

5 Match the phrasal verbs in each sentence (1–6) with their meanings (a–f).

1 A dangerous criminal broke out of prison last night. ☐
2 He was chased by prison guards, but managed to steal a car and get away. ☐
3 The police have found out that he has a forged passport. ☐
4 They believe he caught a plane which took off from Heathrow early this morning. ☐
5 They think that he may turn up in Brazil or Argentina. ☐
6 They also think he will come back one day to visit his family. ☐

a discovered
b appear
c not be caught
d escaped from
e return
f left the ground

Grammar: modal verbs for speculation

6 Match the sentences (1–8) with the different degrees of probability (a–f).

1 The lights are on inside the house. James must be in. ☐ *b*
2 He might be in the shower. That's why he isn't answering the door. ☐
3 He could be ill and can't get out of bed. ☐
4 He may have gone out and simply left the lights on. ☐
5 He can't have gone out. That's his car in the driveway. ☐
6 There's someone moving around upstairs. It must be him. ☐
7 It can't be him. He's much taller than that. ☐
8 A burglar must have broken in! ☐

a (present tense) It's possible that this is true.
b (present tense) It's certain that this is true.
c (present tense) It's certainly not true.
d (past tense) It's possible that this happened.
e (past tense) It's certain that this happened.
f (past tense) This definitely didn't happen.

7 Read the questions and write speculative answers. Use the modal verbs from Exercise 6.

Who is the woman in Leonardo Da Vinci's painting *The Mona Lisa*?

1 'There are no records to show that he was married, so I'm sure it isn't his wife.'
It can't ....
2 'I'm sure it's Lisa del Giocondo. That's who historians think it is.'
It ....
3 'Her face is like Da Vinci's face. Perhaps it's a self-portrait.'
It ....

How did Van Gogh lose his ear?

4 'I'm sure he cut it off himself.'
He ....
5 'It's possible that it was his friend, Gauguin, who cut it off.'
It ....
6 'Perhaps it was an accident.'
It ....

8 Complete the text with the verbs in brackets and the correct modal form of *may, might must* or *could*. More than one answer may be possible.

The Mystery of Shakespeare's Identity

Did William Shakespeare really exist? If so, did he really write all his plays himself? These ¹..................... (seem) like strange questions to ask about the greatest writer in history. However, some experts believe that one man ²..................... (not write) so many plays and poems on his own. They argue that this was impossible, and say that he ³..................... (have) help from other writers. There are also historians who believe that the man named William Shakespeare, who lived in Stratford-upon-Avon, was not Shakespeare the writer because he had never been abroad. Therefore, he ⁴..................... (know) about the places and people described in Shakespeare's plays. Consequently, they believe that the real Shakespeare ⁵..................... (be) an aristocrat who had travelled widely. In universities all over the world, academics today are doing more research into Shakespeare's true identity. It ⁶..................... (take) many years to solve the mystery. On the other hand, they ⁷..................... (never / find out) the truth.

6B Art mysteries

Reading

1 Read the article about the Titanic. Match the headings (a–d) with the paragraphs (1–3). There is one extra heading.

a Why were so many lives lost?
b Myths and legends
c Stories of the survivors
d Human error or bad design?

The mystery of the Titanic

When the Titanic left Southampton for New York in April 1912, it was the largest, most luxurious ship that had ever been built. Its owners even said that they had built a ship that was 'unsinkable'. However, just four days into its maiden voyage, the Titanic and 1,523 passengers and crew were lost forever under the freezing waters of the Atlantic Ocean. How did such a terrible disaster happen? The fact is that nobody knows the whole story.

1 ....

What we do know is that just before midnight, on 11th April 1912, the huge ship hit an iceberg. As it sank, the Titanic broke in two. This means that there must have been a serious problem with the ship's design. Another problem was the old-fashioned rudder. By the time the lookouts had seen the iceberg, it was too late to *steer* the enormous ship away from disaster. The Titanic might have been able to turn more quickly if its rudder had been larger and more modern. Another story is that the Titanic's radio operators did not pass on iceberg warnings to the captain. This might be true, as evidence shows that

two ships in the area sent early reports of icebergs to the Titanic. The question is: did the captain ever receive them?

2 ....

But there are other stranger theories about the Titanic, such as the legend of the mummy's curse. According to this story, the Egyptian mummy of the Princess of Amen-Ra was brought secretly on board the Titanic by her new owner, an American who had bought her in London and wanted to take her to New York. The mummy had a terrible curse on her and brought terror and death wherever she went. This story is probably a myth since there is no evidence of a mummy ever being put *on* board the ship. However, the lid of the Princess' coffin was sold to the British Museum, where it is to this day. So, one question remains: what happened to the mummy and its coffin?

3 ....

One of the main reasons why so many people died is that there were not enough lifeboats for everybody. But the ship had been designed to carry enough lifeboats,

so why were they never fitted? One theory is that this was to allow more room for people to walk along the deck. At first, many of the passengers did not want to get into the lifeboats. The ship was sinking slowly and they may not have understood how much danger they were in. Strangely, although another ship, the SS Californian, which was less than 19 miles away, saw the Titanic's distress signal, it did not act immediately. Eventually, another ship, RMS Carpathia, came to rescue survivors, but it arrived too late. Of the 2,228 passengers and crew members on board, only 705 people survived.

---

2 Read the text again. Are the sentences true or false?

	T	F
1 The Titanic's owners believed the ship couldn't sink.	☐	☐
2 The Titanic hit the iceberg because the rudder was too large.	☐	☐
3 The captain may not have received radio warnings about icebergs in the area.	☐	☐
4 Records show that an Egyptian mummy was hidden on board the Titanic.	☐	☐
5 There wasn't enough room on the deck to put the necessary number of lifeboats.	☐	☐
6 The Titanic sank very quickly and there were no other ships near enough to help.	☐	☐
7 1,523 people didn't survive the sinking of the Titanic.	☐	☐

64

Listening

3 🔊 **6.1** Listen to an interview with an expert on the mysteries of the Atlantic Ocean. Match the names (1–3) with the places (A–D) on the map. There is one extra place.

1 The Bermuda Triangle ☐
2 The Lost City of Atlantis ☐
3 The Titanic ☐

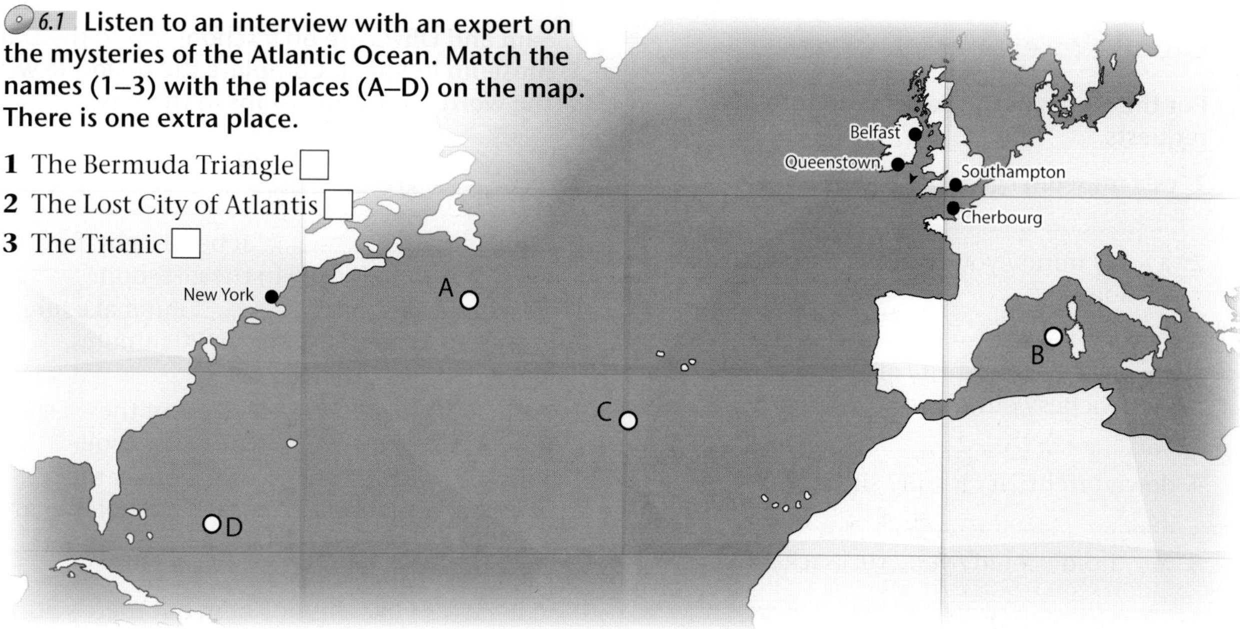

Belfast
Queenstown
Southampton
Cherbourg
New York
A ○
B ○
C ○
○ D

4 **Read the questions carefully and listen again. Choose the correct option (a, b or c).**

1 Why does the radio presenter talk about the Titanic first?
   a because it is his favourite mystery
   b because it happened in the Atlantic
   c because it is a mystery that has recently been solved

2 What was special about Atlantis?
   a The people were very imaginative.
   b Its society was more advanced than other societies.
   c Its people could control the climate.

3 What did the people of Atlantis do to anger the gods?
   a They stopped believing in them.
   b They were no longer good and honest.
   c They used too much technology.

4 What happened to the island of Santorini?
   a It disappeared into the sea.
   b It was destroyed by a volcano.
   c It was destroyed by earthquakes.

5 According to Plato, when was Atlantis destroyed?
   a 3,600 years ago
   b more than 11,000 years ago
   c the date is unknown

6 What causes planes to disappear over the Bermuda Triangle?
   a aliens
   b natural causes
   c no explanation has been found

Grammar: second conditional

5 **Match the sentence beginnings (1–5) with the endings (a–e).**

1 If I went on a cruise in the Atlantic, ☐
2 If explorers stopped visiting the wreck of the Titanic, ☐
3 If I had to fly over the Bermuda Triangle, ☐
4 If there were alien spaceships flying over the Atlantic, ☐
5 If the lost city of Atlantis was rediscovered, ☐

a it would suffer less damage.
b they would be visible to other aircraft.
c I would feel completely terrified!
d I would be worried about icebergs.
e scientists would be very excited.

6 **Complete the sentences with the correct form of the verbs in brackets.**

1 If you .... (decide) to sell your paintings, I .... (buy) some of them.
2 If we .... (buy) an original work of art, we .... (hang) it in the hall.
3 If we .... (win) a lot of money, we .... (go) on a trip round the world.
4 If everyone .... (help) to paint the walls, it .... (not take) long to decorate the house.
5 If nobody .... (want) to be a teacher, who .... (teach) our children?
6 If we .... (have) a bigger car, there .... (be) more room for everybody.

6C Requests

Useful expressions

1 Put the words in the correct order to make requests.

1 we / museum / go / the / today / to / Dalí / can /?

....

2 a / do / mind / you / waiting / moment / for / outside /?

....

3 ate / be / it / would / if / all / right / we / sandwiches / our / here /?

....

4 down / right / if / is / all / sit / I / it /?

....

5 me / hold / could / you / rucksack / for / my /?

....

6 I / could/ look / those / please / ceramic / have / pots, / a / at /?

....

7 me / photo / can / you / of / take / a /?

....

2 Match the responses (a–g) with the requests (1–7) in Exercise 1.

a Yes, of course. My legs are tired too. ☐

b Sorry, I'm really bad at taking photos. ☐

c No, not at all. ☐

d Yes, sure. We can go this afternoon. ☐

e I'm sorry. You can't bring food in here. ☐

f Yes, sure. Why don't you give me your coat as well? ☐

g Yes, of course. I'll get them down for you. ☐

3 Match the requests (1–6) with the places (a–f).

1 Do you mind helping me move this exhibit? ☐

2 Is it all right if I look at those posters, please? ☐

3 Would it be all right if I borrowed more than three books? ☐

4 Could you take a photo of me and my friend in front of the cathedral? ☐

5 Could I order a copy of Ian McEwan's new novel, please? ☐

6 Can you help me find a nice watercolour as a present for my dad? ☐

a gift shop

b bookshop

c art gallery

d museum

e the street

f public library

4 Sam and Olivia are on a school trip to the Dalí museum in Spain. Complete the dialogue with the words and expressions in the box.

can you	could	do you mind	I'm sorry
not at all	of course	would	

Olivia: [1]...................... it be all right if we went and looked in the gift shop?

Teacher: Yes, [2]...................... But make sure you meet back here in 20 minutes.

Olivia: OK. Thanks, sir.

Sam: [*in the gift shop*] Look at these Dalí keyrings. They're really cool!

Olivia: Hmm, they're OK. I prefer the watches. [3]...................... holding my coat while I have a look at them?

Sam: No, [4]...................... .

Olivia: I like this one best, but there's no price.

Sam: I'll ask the assistant ... Excuse me, [5]...................... you tell us the price of the Dalí watches, please?

Assistant: They're €40 each.

Olivia: Oh dear! I haven't got enough cash. [6]...................... lend me €20? I'll pay you back tomorrow.

Sam: [7]......................, I've only got €10 left.

5 Complete the dialogue with the questions and responses (a–g) in the box.

a Can you tell me the price of those cakes, please?

b Could you get me one of those and an orange juice, please?

c Do you mind looking after my stuff while I see what they've got?

d Do you mind waiting a moment while I get it?

e I'm sorry, but I'll have to serve the other customers first.

f Can we go to the café before we look at any more exhibits?

g Not at all.

Ian: I'm really thirsty. [1]...........................

Sally: Good idea! Let's sit at this free table.

Ian: Actually, I'm a bit hungry as well. [2]...........................

Sally: [3]........................... I can see some nice chocolate cakes at the counter. [4]...........................

Ian: Sure. I'll be right back.

Ian: [*at the counter*] Excuse me. [5]...........................

Assistant: They're £2.50 each.

Ian: OK. I'll take two cakes and two orange juices, please.

Assistant: That's £9.50.

Ian: Oh, I've left my money at the table. [6]...........................

Assistant: [7]........................... You'll have to join the back of the queue again.

6 What would you say in each of the situations (1–5)? Choose the best option (a, b or c).

1 You are in an art gallery. You want to know if you can take photos. What do you say to the attendant?

   a Could I take a photo of me, please?

   b Is it all right if I take a photo?

   c Do you mind taking photos, please?

2 You are in a library. You want to leave some books at the desk while you look in another section. What do you say to the assistant?

   a Do you mind helping me with these books?

   b Could you tell me where to find the books, please?

   c Would it be all right if I left these books here for a while?

3 Your friend has asked you to lend her your English dictionary, but you need it to do your homework. How do you respond?

   a Not at all.

   b I'm sorry, I'm using it at the moment.

   c Yes, of course.

4 You haven't finished your art homework and you have to hand it in today. What do you say to your teacher?

   a Do you mind helping me with this?

   b Is it all right if I give it to you tomorrow?

   c Can you wait for me?

5 You're in the school computer room at lunchtime and you're feeling hungry. What do you say to the computer technician?

   a Can you give me some lunch?

   b Do you mind getting me something to eat?

   c Would it be all right if I ate my sandwiches in here?

Pronunciation: words containing *au*

7 🔘 6.2 Say the words in each pair. Is the pronunciation of *au* the same or different? Circle the correct answer. Then listen and check.

1	astronaut	caught	same / different
2	audience	autobiography	same / different
3	audition	because	same / different
4	Australia	cause	same / different
5	author	aunt	same / different
6	autograph	saucer	same / different
7	sausage	daughter	same / different

Writing: an apology

8 Read the notice and the email. Match the questions (1–3) with the answers (a–d). There is one extra answer.

1 Why did the library have to close? ☐

2 How long did the library stay closed for? ☐

3 What happened as a consequence of the snow? ☐

   a There was no electricity.

   b Because of the terrible weather

   c Library staff could not get to work.

   d Until the following day

Notice

Due to the severe weather conditions, the public library will be closed until further notice.

Dear library users,
As a result of yesterday's snow storm, the electricity supply to the library was cut off for several hours. As a result, we were unable to open to the public until today. We apologise for any inconvenience this may have caused.
Margaret Ward, Chief librarian

9 Complete the pairs of sentences so that they have the same meaning. Use *as a result* or *due to*.

1 a It rained heavily yesterday. ...., the school barbecue took place in the main hall.

   b The school barbecue took place in the main hall .... the heavy rain.

2 a The sponsored run has been cancelled .... the hot weather.

   b The weather is too hot. ...., the sponsored run has been cancelled.

3 a The stage collapsed during the show. ...., two students were taken to hospital.

   b Two students were taken to hospital .... the stage collapsing during the show.

10 Choose one of the situations in Exercise 9. Write a short apology to put on the school website. Give an explanation and/or more details of what happened. Use the email in Exercise 8 to help you.

Listening

1 **6.3** You will hear someone talk about her job. Listen and choose the correct option (a–c).

a The woman is a history teacher.

b The woman works in a museum.

c The woman is a tourist guide.

2 **6.4** You will hear an art student talk about how he spends his time when he is not at college. Listen and choose the correct option (a–c).

a The student works on his sculpture.

b The student works as a volunteer.

c The student works in an art gallery.

Reading

3 Match the signs (a–d) with the places (1–5). There is one extra place.

a
Sale!
50% off

b
Do not touch the items on display.
Please ask for assistance.

c
Guided tours every hour.
Next tour starts here at   3.15 p.m.

d
Student Art Display
In the main hall.
Open all day.

1 in a museum
2 in a school
3 in a library
4 in a bookshop
5 in a gift shop

Word list / Unit 6

abstract (adj)	....		landscape (n)	....
adapt (v)	....		lead a double life (phr)	....
appeal (v)	....		lifeboat (n)	....
apply (v)	....		lookout (n)	....
argue (v)	....		maiden (adj)	....
argument (n)	....		mystery (n)	....
attendant (n)	....		novel (n)	....
bizarre (adj)	....		observer (n)	....
collapse (v)	....		obsess ed with (adj)	....
collector (n)	....		on board (phr)	....
consequence (n)	....		page-turner (n)	....
cookery book (n)	....		parallel (adj)	....
crew (n)	....		plot (n)	....
crop circle (n)	....		reference book (n)	....
cruise (n)	....		regarded as (adj)	....
curse (n)	....		release	....
distress signal (n)	....		rudder (n)	....
drawing (n)	....		sculptor (n)	....
embarrassing (adj)	....		sculpture (n)	....
entrance (n)	....		still life (n)	....
explanation (n)	....		struggle (n)	....
extra-terrestrial (n)	....		stuff (n)	....
fake (n & adj)	....		survive (v)	....
flame (n)	....		survivor (n)	....
flatten (v)	....		suspect (n)	....
fool (v)	....		thriller (n)	....
forgery (n)	....		unsinkable	....
genre (n)	....		value (n)	....
hoax	....		victim (n)	....
iceberg (n)	....		watercolour (n)	....
identity (n)	....			
inconvenience (n)	....			
innocent (n)	....			

Grammar Practice | Unit 6

modal verbs for speculation

We use the modal verbs *may, might, could, can't, couldn't* and *must* to speculate or guess about an event or situation. *May, might* and *could* all show that we think the explanation is possible; *can't* and *couldn't* show that we think it is impossible; and *must* shows that we think it is probable or perhaps almost certain.

> Notice that we do not normally use *can* to speculate, and we never use *mustn't*; we normally use *couldn't* only for speculation about the past.

When we speculate about the present, the modals are followed by a **bare infinitive**.

(Situation: I don't know where my mobile phone is.)
It may/might/could be on the table in the hall. (It's possible.)

When we speculate about the past, the modals are followed by a **bare perfect infinitive** – that is, *have* + **past participle** of the main verb.

(Situation: I don't know why my friend didn't come to football practice.)
He must have had something really important to do. (It's probable.)

speculative questions

We can form speculative questions using *could*, to ask whether a particular answer/explanation is possible or not. We put *could* before the subject, followed by a **normal bare infinitive** for the present, or a **bare perfect infinitive** for the past.
Could John be innocent? (Is it possible that he is?)
Could John have stolen the money? (Is it possible that he did?)

We can also begin speculative questions with question words such as *What, Why, Where, How*, etc.
What could that strange noise be?

1 **Circle the correct option.**

Where's my purse? I know I(can't)/ mustn't have lost it.

1 Joe looks very happy. He *couldn't / must* have passed his exam.
2 Emma isn't here – I suppose she *may / can* have missed the bus.
3 Everything's wet – it must *rain / have rained* last night.
4 He ate only an hour ago, so he can't *feel / have felt* hungry again.
5 Holly *couldn't / mustn't* have done such a terrible thing – it's just not possible!

2 **Write sentences with the correct modal verb to speculate about each situation.**

Julia isn't at school today.
a She's at the dentist's. (**?**)
She may be at the dentist's.
b She's gone on a school trip. (✗)
She can't have gone on a school trip.
c She's ill. (✓)
She must be ill.

1 My mobile phone isn't working.
a It's broken. (✗)
....
b It got wet. (**?**)
....
c The battery needs charging. (✓)
....

2 I can't find my jeans.
a They're in the washing machine. (**?**)
....
b They've been stolen. (✗)
....
c My sister is wearing them. (✓)
....

3 **Complete the dialogues with *may/might/could, can't* or *must* and the correct form of the verb in brackets.**

A: Oh no! Someone's eaten my bowl of ice cream!
B: Look, the cat's got ice cream on her whiskers. She *must have eaten* (eat) it.

A: Mum, where's the TV remote?
B: Well, it ¹...................... (disappear) on its own. You've been using it all evening.
A: I guess it ²...................... (fall) down the back of the sofa ... No, it isn't here.
B: I know – you went into the kitchen a minute ago, didn't you? You ³...................... (leave) it there.

A: What's the matter? Why are you crying?
B: I fell off the ladder and I think I ⁴...................... (break) my wrist.
A: Let me see. No, I'm sure it ⁵...................... (be) broken. It's badly sprained though – it ⁶...................... (be) very painful.

70

4 Rewrite the second sentence using could, so that it means the same as the first.

I wonder who that is.
Who *could that be?*

1 I can't imagine what made her so angry.
What ....

2 I have no idea where my trainers are.
Where ....

3 I can't understand how I made such a stupid mistake.
How ....

4 I really don't know who is trying to get me into trouble.
Who ....

second conditional

We use the second conditional to talk about an imaginary action, situation or result which depends on an imaginary condition – not a real condition – in the present and/or future.

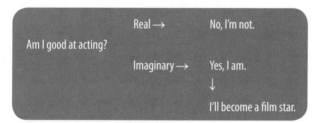

If I was good at acting, I'd become a film star.

We form the second conditional with *If* + **past simple** for the condition, followed by *would/ wouldn't* + **bare infinitive** for the resulting action or situation.

We can also use *could/couldn't* or *might/ mightn't* instead of *would*, but *would* is more common.

We can put the two parts of the sentence in any order, but notice that when the sentence begins with the condition, we must put a comma between the condition and the result.
If I had any money (condition), *I'd lend you some* (result).
I would learn to drive (result) *if I was old enough* (condition).

> Notice that the use of the past simple in the condition does not show completed action – it shows an imaginary or hypothetical situation.

5 Circle the correct option.

I *'ll* / *'d* be much better at sports if I *didn't* / *wouldn't* wear glasses.

1 If I *didn't have* / *hadn't* a test tomorrow, I *won't* / *wouldn't* be studying tonight.

2 Jerry *hadn't* / *wouldn't* be so unfit if he *walks* / *walked* to school.

3 If you *bought* / *would buy* a car, I *could teach* / *taught* you how to drive.

4 I *wasn't* / *wouldn't be* good at French if I *didn't* / *wouldn't* like it.

5 If I *wanted* / *would want* to tell a friend some exciting news, I *would send* / *sent* them a text message.

questions in the second conditional

We form questions in the second conditional by putting the modal (*would*, *could* or *might*) before the subject.
***Would** you be happy if you were famous?*
We can also begin questions with question words such as *What, Why, Where, How*, etc.
***What would** you do if you were me?*
Notice that the question is always in the result clause, even when the sentence begins with the *if* clause.
*If you were famous, **would** you be happy?*

6 Write questions. Use the second conditional.

If you / miss / the last bus, how / you / get / home /?

If you missed the last bus, how would you get home? /

1 You / lend / someone your new camera if you / not need / it yourself /?
....

2 If you / win / the lottery, what / you / do / with the money /?
....

3 Why / anyone / buy / a car if they / not know / how to drive /?
....

4 If you / can / travel / anywhere in the world, where / you / go /?
....

5 If a shop assistant / give / you too much change, / you / keep / the extra money /?
....

Review Units 5 and 6

Grammar review: *a, an, the* or (–)

1 Complete the sentences with *a, an, the* or no article (–).

1 Have you seen .... new film by James Cameron yet?
2 Sam got .... new bike for his birthday.
3 I like this shop. .... assistants are helpful and friendly.
4 Is Mark still in .... shower?
5 I think Johnny Depp is .... excellent actor.
6 Alex takes .... dog for a long walk every evening.
7 Do you enjoy swimming in .... sea?
8 .... drum is a percussion instrument.
9 We're raising money to help .... poor in Africa.
10 The Hebrides are a group of islands in .... Scotland.

1 mark per item: ...... / 10 marks

Passive

2 Write sentences and questions with the correct form of the passive.

1 When / the city of Petra / build / ?
....
2 Atlantis / destroy / earthquakes / thousands of years ago.
....
3 Those paintings / still / not restore.
....
4 The students / not give / their exam results yet.
....
5 Where / coffee / usually / grow / ?
....

2 marks per item: ...... / 10 marks

3 Complete the sentences with *can, can't, must, will* or *won't* + the correct passive form of the verb.

1 Dinner .... (serve) in an hour.
2 The artefacts .... (take) out of the museum.
3 Children .... (accompany) by an adult at all times.
4 Your order .... (not deliver) until next Monday.
5 .... (these glasses / wash) in the dishwasher or will they break?

1 mark per item: ...... / 5 marks

must and *can't*

4 Complete the sentences with *must* or *can't* and the correct form of the verbs in brackets.

1 That man over there .... (be) Molly's dad. He's too young.
2 The cake is burnt! I .... (put) the oven on too high.
3 The children are tired. It .... (be) time for them to go to bed.
4 Paula .... (go) home because her bag is still here.
5 The sheep have got out of the field. Somebody .... (leave) the gate open.
6 I can't believe you've finished all the sandwiches! You .... (be) hungry!

1 mark per item: ...... / 6 marks

Second conditional

5 Write second conditional sentences.

1 If / I / win / the lottery /, / give / some money / charity.
....
2 He / play / a lot better / if / practise / more.
....
3 If / you / go / Italy / , / visit / Rome?
....
4 Van Gogh / be / very rich / if / alive today.
....
5 If / Lisa / do / some exercise / , / feel /much healthier.
....

2 marks per item: ...... / 10 marks

6 Complete the gaps in the text with one word.

For my birthday last year, I [1]...................... given six months' membership at the best gym in town. It was [2]...................... present from my sister and it [3]...................... have been cheap. [4]...................... gym has two fitness rooms as well as [5]...................... pool, but that's not all. My sister says there are plans to build some squash courts next year, and there might [6]...................... a new sauna and jacuzzi as well. [7]...................... problem is that I never have any free time to go there! If I [8]...................... there two or three times a week, I [9]...................... be a lot fitter than I am now. I'll try to go tomorrow after school.

1 mark per item: ...... / 9 marks

Vocabulary review: describing objects

7 Complete the sentences with the words in the box.

| brick | concrete | leather | plastic | wood | wool |

1 All my baby sister's toys are made of brightly-coloured ....

2 The house was in the middle of the forest and entirely made of ....

3 Sheep are valuable animals because they produce ....

4 When I ride my motorbike, I wear a .... jacket and trousers for protection.

5 The bridge was built of huge, grey, ... blocks and was very strong.

6 I loved the red .... houses in town.

1 mark per item: ...... / 6 marks

8 Write the descriptions. Put the words in the correct order.

1 mummy / a(n) / ancient / Egyptian

....

2 huge / a(n) / steel / sculpture / amazing

....

3 a / silk / dress / beautiful / red

....

4 immense / oval / stadium / a(n) / football

....

5 wonderful / black-and-white / film / old / a(n)

....

2 marks per item: ...... / 10 marks

Art and books

9 Circle the correct option.

1 *Romeo and Juliet* is Shakespeare's most famous ....

   a play   **b** poetry   **c** novel

2 Van Gogh painted a .... of himself with a bandaged ear.

   a landscape   **b** still life   **c** portrait

3 I find other people's lives fascinating, so I love reading ....

   a autobiographies   **b** classic novels
   c historical novels

4 I think that some .... can be better than the original painting!

   a fakes   **b** hoaxes   **c** forgeries

5 I think .... art is more interesting than paintings that are very realistic.

   a watercolour   **b** abstract   **c** picture

1 mark per item: ...... / 5 marks

Prepositions

10 Complete the sentences with the correct form of a verb from box A and a preposition from box B.

A
| complain | do | find | get | have | pay | run |
| take | think | turn |

B
| about (×2) | away | for | into | off | on |
| out (×2) | up |

1 Oh no! We've .... of salt. I'll go and buy some more.

2 I wish to .... the terrible service in your restaurant.

3 Can I .... the tickets by credit card?

4 The robbers .... with six million pounds.

5 The plane .... from Amsterdam airport at six o'clock.

6 Punk and hip-hop .... an influence ...... my music.

7 We need to .... research .... genetic diseases.

8 Have you .... what to wear to the party?

9 I've just .... that it's Tim's birthday today. I had no idea!

10 Sandra always .... late for class.

2 marks per item: ...... / 20 marks

11 Communicate

Complete the dialogue with the words in the box.

| because | could | I'll | looking |
| not | right | to | what | why |

Tim: [1]........... do you need that huge bag for?

Anne: [2]........... put all my clothes and stuff in.

Tim: But we're only there for two days. [3]........... do you need so much?

Anne: [4]........... I need light clothes for hot weather and warm clothes for cold weather and ...

Tim: OK! Let's get on the train before it leaves!

Anne: Sure. [5]........... you hold my bag for me while I get on?

Tim: Yes, sure. [6]........... pass it up to you.

Anne: Is it all [7]........... if we sit here, by the window?

Tim: Yes, of course. Actually, I'm really thirsty. Do you mind [8]........... after my bag while I go and get a drink?

Anne: [9]........... at all. Could you get me a coke, please?

Tim: Sure. Large or small?

1 mark per item: ...... / 9 marks

Total: ...... / 100 marks

7A Cracking the code

Vocabulary: science and technology

1 Read the definitions and complete the crossword.

Across

4 a place with lots of scientific equipment where scientists work

5 a test that scientists do in order to discover if their theories are true

6 detailed study of something in order to discover new information about it

Down

1 information, especially facts or figures

2 a completely new and different idea or way of doing something

3 a mechanical device or instrument

2 Complete the sentences with the words in the box.

> applications   discovery   knowledge
> results   test   theory

1 Crick and Watson were the first scientists to publish a .... about the structure of DNA.

2 Rosalind Franklin shared the .... of her work with Crick and Watson.

3 DNA has many different ...., especially in medicine and forensic science.

4 Fleming's .... of penicillin was one of the most important in medical history.

5 Rejewski's .... of cryptology helped him to crack the enigma code.

6 Scientists have to .... new medicines before they can be given to patients.

Working with words: prefixes

3 Write the opposite forms of the verbs.

1 appear   ....
2 pack   ....
3 connect   ....
4 encode   ....
5 lock   ....
6 agree   ....

4 Complete the sentences with the correct form of the verbs in Exercise 3.

1 Jill .... her suitcase as soon as she arrived at her hotel.

2 It is not easy to .... the symbols on Egyptian tombs.

3 Everyone .... that this year's exam had been more difficult than last year's.

4 It's a good idea to .... your computer during a bad storm.

5 I think I've got the wrong key. I can't .... the door!

6 The dinosaurs .... from the Earth millions of years ago.

5 Circle the correct option.

1 This programme will *disable / enable* you to create 3D images.

2 The experiment has failed. We'll need to *undo / redo* it.

3 These *enlarged / endangered* photos of wild animals would make fantastic posters.

4 My watch, which I lost last month, suddenly *disappeared / reappeared* yesterday.

5 After the earthquake, the city had to be *recreated / rebuilt*.

6 We've *rewritten / renamed* all the files because their original filenames were too long.

Grammar: third conditional

6 Write sentences about the pictures. Use the prompts to help you.

1 Tania / take an umbrella / not get wet.

....
....
....

2 John / not fall asleep / not get sunburnt.

....
....
....

3 The pan / not catch fire / someone / turn off the gas.

....
....
....

4 Anna / not order pasta / know portions / be so large.

....
....
....

5 Tim and Max / not go to the cinema / realise / it was a romantic film.

....
....
....

6 You / drive more carefully / we / not have an accident.

....
....
....

7 Match the beginnings of the sentences (1–5) with the endings (a–e).

1 If I had passed all my exams, ☐
2 The students wouldn't have been punished ☐
3 Would scientists have developed nuclear energy ☐
4 If dinosaurs had not died out, ☐
5 I wouldn't have lost all my work ☐

a if they had listened to the teacher.
b would human beings have existed?
c I would have gone to university.
d if the computer hadn't crashed.
e if Oppenheimer hadn't split the atom?

8 Complete the quote.

'If God .... (intend) us to fly, he .... (give) us wings.'

Father of the Wright brothers

9 Complete the sentences with the correct form of the verb in brackets.

1 If Gutenberg .... (not invent) his printing machine, ordinary people .... (not be able) to read books and newspapers.

2 If Columbus .... (not discover) America, Europeans .... (not have) potatoes or tomatoes in their diet.

3 If Marco Polo .... (not travel) to China, he .... (not take) noodles back to Italy.

4 If the Italians .... (not know) about noodles, ... (they / learn) how to make spaghetti?

5 If the Wright brothers .... (listen) to their father, they .... (not be) the first men to fly a plane.

6 If Dr Percy Spencer .... (not invent) the microwave oven, I .... (learn) how to cook properly.

Reading

1 Read the text about Joan of Arc and answer the questions.

1 Where did Joan of Arc grow up?
2 Who told her to join the army?
3 How old was she when she died?

Joan of Arc

Milla Jovovich stars in Luc Besson's 1999 film, *The Messenger: The Story of Joan of Arc*

Joan of Arc is one of the great female rebel leaders in history. There are lots of books and films about her. ¹..................... She has also been the subject of great paintings and statues around the world. So, why does everyone remember the story of Joan of Arc? ²..................... Even today, she is a symbol of French freedom and independence.

When Joan was born, in 1412, France was in the middle of the Hundred Years' War. The north of the country, where Joan lived, was ruled by the English. ³..................... From the age of twelve, Joan began to hear voices and see visions from God. When she was sixteen, the voices told her to join Charles' army and drive the English out of France. So, Joan dressed herself as a boy and travelled to Orleans, to the royal court. She asked the Duke to let her become a knight and lead the army. ⁴.....................

When she joined the army, Joan cut her hair short and wore men's armour. ⁵..................... Because she believed God was with her, Joan was a great military leader. She was never afraid to attack, even when the French army was smaller than the English one. The French army won many battles and took back the major cities of Orleans and Paris.

In 1431, Joan was caught by the English and thrown into prison. When Joan told them about her visions from God, they didn't believe her and thought she was a witch. On 30 May, 1431, aged just 19, Joan was burned to death. ⁶..................... However, Joan of Arc refused to take back what she had said and died as bravely as she had gone into battle.

2 Match the sentences (a–f) with the gaps (1–6).

a The rest of France was ruled by Duke Charles of Orleans.

b Perhaps it is because her actions changed French history.

c She appears in works by Shakespeare and Voltaire, and Verdi wrote an opera about her.

d Perhaps she could have escaped such a horrible death if she had kept quiet about her visions.

e She was afraid that if she looked like a girl, the soldiers would not listen to her.

f Normally, he would not have agreed, but he was desperate to free France from the English.

3 Complete the sentences with words from the text.

1 If Joan of Arc hadn't changed French ...., she might not be remembered today.

2 Would Joan of Arc have become a symbol of French .... if she hadn't died young?

3 The Duke of Orleans would not have made her the .... of the army if he hadn't been desperate.

4 If Joan of Arc hadn't .... to take back what she said about her visions, she might not have been killed.

Vocabulary: politics

4 Complete the texts with the words in the boxes.

> campaign   democracy   election   policies   right   vote

1

In countries where there is a(n) ¹...................., everybody over the age of 18 has the ².................... to ³.................... for their favourite political party. Before a(n) ⁴...................., each party runs a(n) ⁵..................... They try to persuade people that their ⁶.................... are the best, especially on education, health and the environment.

> freedom   government   law   politics   protest

2

In certain countries around the world, the ¹.................... does not allow people the ².................... to express different views about ³..................... In fact, it is often against the ⁴.................... to openly criticise them. Anyone who organises a ⁵.................... may be arrested and thrown into jail.

Listening

5 🔊 **7.1** Listen to Matt and Ella talking about Rosa Parks. Choose the best caption from the options (a–d) for each of the photos (1–2).

a Rosa worked for the city bus company.
b Rosa travelled to work by bus.
c Rosa broke the law and was arrested.
d Rosa was sent to prison for almost a year.

6 Listen again. Are the sentences true or false?

	T	F
1 In the 1950s, African Americans were not allowed to travel by bus.	☐	☐
2 Rosa didn't give up her seat on the bus because she was asleep.	☐	☐
3 American civil rights leaders heard Rosa's story and decided to help her.	☐	☐
4 During the protest, African Americans refused to sit at the back of the bus.	☐	☐
5 Their campaign was successful because it affected the city's economy.	☐	☐
6 Rosa worked for the civil rights movement until her death.	☐	☐
7 She was awarded a medal in 2005.	☐	☐

Grammar: *could/should have done*

7 Complete the sentences with *could, couldn't, should* or *shouldn't.*

1 According to the law at the time, Rosa Parks .... have given up her seat.
2 She .... have gone to prison, but she was asked to pay a fine instead.
3 Rosa .... have known that she would become famous.
4 Rosa needed help with the campaign. She .... have organised such a big protest on her own.
5 The campaign meant that city businesses .... have lost a lot of money.
6 Do you think that Rosa .... have broken the law?

8 Complete the dialogues with *could / couldn't have* and *should/shouldn't have* and the correct form of the verbs in brackets.

A: Are you still waiting for Jim?
B: Yes. He *should have been* (be) here an hour ago!

1 A: Someone has stolen my bag!
B: Well, you .... (put) it on the back of your chair!

2 A: I feel really cold.
B: You .... (bring) a jumper with you.

3 A: Fiona's coming to see us today and she's bringing the new baby.
B: Oh, no! I .... (buy) her a present.

4 A: Lucy .... (tell) Chris about the party.
B: I agree. He was the only one who didn't know about it.

5 A: I think Andy has taken my jacket by mistake.
B: No, it .... (be) Andy. He didn't take his coat off all evening.

6 A: I can't find my football gloves anywhere!
B: You .... (leave) them at the club after the match. Why don't you ring them and ask if they're still there?

Regrets and criticisms

Useful expressions

1 Read the sentences and decide if they express criticism (**C**) or regret (**R**).

	C	R
1 I wish I had studied art at school.	☐	☐
2 I wish you hadn't told the children that story.	☐	☐
3 You shouldn't have bought that top.	☐	☐
4 I wish I hadn't said that to Carol!	☐	☐
5 I should have paid more attention in class.	☐	☐
6 My parents should have made me practise more.	☐	☐

2 Match the criticisms and regrets (1–6) in Exercise 1 with the sentences (a–f) below.

a I don't know if she'll ever be my friend again.

b I could have been a professional musician by now.

c They're going to have bad dreams all night!

d Then I would have passed my exams.

e It doesn't suit you.

f But I chose to do science instead.

3 Complete the dialogue with the words in the box.

had	have	should (×2)	shouldn't	wish

Ian: I ¹..................... I'd remembered Tilly's birthday. Now she isn't talking to me.

Alice: Did you apologise to her?

Ian: Not really. You see, I was really busy and ...

Alice: That's not an excuse! You ²..................... have forgotten your girlfriend's birthday!

Ian: I know, but ...

Alice: You ³..................... at least have sent her a card. That would have helped.

Ian: I know. I could ⁴..................... bought one the other day, when I was in town. I just didn't think.

Alice: I wish you ⁵..................... told me it was her birthday. I could have helped you to organise a party or something.

Ian: I know. I'm really sorry.

Alice: You ⁶..................... have said that to Tilly when you had the chance!

4 Write sentences with the words to complete the cartoon story about Sara and Ben. Add any other necessary words.

1 I / wish / not split up / Ben / last week!

....

....

I really miss him!

2 I / should / not spend / all that time at the party / dancing / my friends.

....

....

He must have felt left out.

3 I went over to talk to him, but I didn't realise he was upset.

he / could / just tell me / want to go home.

....

....

4 Then we had a terrible argument.
I wish / we not argue.

....

....

5 I was so angry that I broke up with him.
I / should / not be / so stupid!

....

....

6 Now he's going out with Tara. It's too late to apologise.
I wish / say sorry / when / have chance!

....

....

Pronunciation: silent letters

5 Read the sentences. How do you pronounce the underlined words?

1 We took our crazy cat to see an animal <u>psychologist</u>.

2 I <u>doubt</u> it'll rain today – just look at that blue sky!

3 Kate threw a water <u>bomb</u> in the classroom.

4 Half of the students in our class joined the <u>campaign</u>.

5 Would you like to visit the <u>castle</u>?

6 The number of <u>foreign</u> visitors to the <u>island</u> has increased.

7 You need a good <u>knowledge</u> of maths if you want to be a <u>scientist</u>.

6 ⊘ 7.2 Listen and check. Practise saying the sentences in Exercise 5.

Writing: a story

7 Read Lucy's story and answer the questions.

a What event did Lucy organise?

b Who helped her?

c What mistakes did she make?

A big barbecue disaster!

Last Saturday morning, my friend Sonia came round to my house. It was such a lovely day that we sat outside in the garden. ¹..................... chatting for a while, we suddenly had a great idea: we could have a barbecue in the garden! I went inside to ask my mum if it was all right ²..................... phoning my friends to invite them round. Quite a lot of them weren't in, so we left messages on their voicemail.

In the afternoon, we went shopping for burgers, sausages, drinks and snacks. ³..................... checking for messages on our mobiles, we made a list of everyone who was coming to the party. My dad helped us ⁴..................... cooking the burgers. Then we realised we didn't have any bread rolls to put them in! I felt like such an idiot! I shouldn't have gone shopping ⁵..................... first making a list! But that wasn't the only mistake I made. Halfway through the party, Sonia told me that everyone was here, but we'd forgotten to invite Chris. I should have written the guest list ⁶..................... making any calls!

8 Now complete the story with the prepositions *after*, *before*, *by* or *without*.

9 Rewrite the pairs of sentences as one sentence. Use the prepositions in brackets.

1 We sat in the garden chatting. Then we phoned our friends. (before)
Before ....

2 We phoned lots of people. We didn't make a guest list first. (without)
We ....

3 We went shopping. We didn't make a shopping list. (before)
We ....

4 We checked our phone messages. Then we made a list of who was coming. (after)
After ....

5 Dad helped us. He did the barbecue. (by)
Dad ....

6 He cooked the meat. Then he realised we hadn't bought any rolls. (after)
After ....

10 Think about a time when you made a mistake. Choose one of the situations (a–d) below or use your own ideas.

a You forgot to do something important.

b You bought a new phone/TV/computer, but didn't read the instructions.

c You got up late and missed an important event.

d You spent all your money.

11 Make notes about your story.

When did it happen?
....
....
Who and what was involved?
....
....
What mistake did you make?
....
....
What happened as a result?
....
....

12 Now write your story. Remember to include some of the prepositions in Exercise 8. Use Lucy's story to help you.

7D Explore More

Reading

1 Match the sentences (a–e) with the gaps (1–4). There is one extra sentence.

> Dear Chris,
>
> I'm really sorry you weren't invited to the barbecue yesterday. ¹...................... We weren't very well organised and did a few silly things. I even forgot to get bread rolls for the burgers! ²...................... You would've enjoyed it if you'd been there. ³...................... Mum says I can invite two or three friends round this evening to help us finish it. Would you like to come? ⁴...................... If the weather stays nice, we'll probably have another barbecue.
>
> Lucy
>
> PS I've sent you a text message as well.

   a I wanted to ask you, but I forgot to phone you.
   b We can go there together.
   c But in the end, it was still quite a good party.
   d However, we've got lots of food left.
   e Sonia and Ian will be there too.

Listening

2 🔘 **7.3** You will hear three speakers. Match the speakers (1–3) with the statements (a–d). There is one extra statement.

   This speaker:
   a has never voted in an election. ....
   b didn't know who to vote for in an election. ....
   c organised a protest. ....
   d has an interest in politics. ....

3 🔘 **7.4** You will hear three speakers. Match the speakers (1–3) with the statements (a–d). There is one extra statement.

   This speaker:
   a visited a large lake in Florida. ....
   b saw alligators on holiday in Florida. ....
   c went to Disney World. ....
   d used to visit family in Florida. ....

Word list Unit 7

account (n)	....	humpback (whale) (n)	....
achieve (v)	....	independence (n)	....
achievement (n)	....	influence (n & v)	....
acknowledge (v)	....	innovation (n)	....
ancestor (n)	....	knight (n)	....
apartheid (n)	....	knowledge (n)	....
application (n)	....	lawyer (n)	....
armour (n)	....	mould (n)	....
award (v)	....	ordinary (adj)	....
battle (n)	....	origins (n pl)	....
bursting with (adj)	....	persuade (v)	....
campaign (n)	....	policy (n)	....
caption (n)	....	political (adj)	....
cipher (n)	....	politics (n pl)	....
come round (phr v)	....	predict (v)	....
contribution (n)	....	punish (v)	....
crack a code (phr)	....	rabies (n uncount)	....
cryptology (n)	....	rebel (n)	....
current (n)	....	research (n)	....
data (n pl)	....	rhinoceros (n)	....
decipher (v)	....	sequence (v)	....
discovery (n)	....	split (v)	....
diversity (n)	....	springbok (n)	....
election (n)	....	tactic (n)	....
equipment (n)	....	thrill	....
essential (adj)	....	unofficial (adj)	....
fault (n)	....	vision (n)	....
forensic science (n)	....	witch (n)	....
freedom (n)	....	work out (phr v)	....
habitat (n)	....		

Grammar Practice — Unit 7

third conditional

We use the third conditional to talk about an imaginary action, event or situation in the past, which depends on an imaginary past condition. The imaginary condition and the resulting action or situation are the opposite of what really happened.

> **What really happened:** *He wasn't careful, so he made a mistake.*
> **Imaginary situation:** *He was careful, so he didn't make a mistake.*
> *If he **had been** careful, he **wouldn't have made** a mistake.*

We form the third conditional with *if* + **past perfect** for the condition, followed by *would/wouldn't* + *have* + **past participle** for the resulting action or situation.

We can also use *could/couldn't* or *might/mightn't* instead of *would/wouldn't*.

We can put the two parts of the sentence in any order, but notice that when the sentence begins with the condition, we must put a comma between the condition and the result.

*If we **had known** about the meeting (condition), we **would have been** there (result).*

1 Complete the third conditional sentences.

If I *had known* (know) you were going to the concert, I *would have gone* (go) with you.

1 You .... (not misunderstand) the instructions if you .... (be) more careful.

2 If Ron .... (not forget) to set his alarm clock, he .... (not oversleep) the next morning.

3 Dan .... (not tease) Fay if he .... (realise) how much he was upsetting her.

4 I .... (send) you a text message if you .... (give) me your mobile number.

5 Joe .... (get) a better mark in the exam if he .... (not be) so nervous.

2 Write third conditional sentences.

Harry didn't make enough food, so his dinner party was a disaster.

If Harry had made enough food, his dinner party wouldn't have been a disaster.

1 Mum had the flu, so she didn't go to work.

....

2 Craig failed the chemistry test because he hadn't studied.

....

3 We didn't tell our parents we'd be late, so they were worried.

....

4 He went to prison because he broke the law.

....

5 Max wrote down the wrong address, so he couldn't find our house.

....

3 Match the situations (1–6) with the results/ reasons (a–f).

1 I stayed up late. [c]
2 I didn't have enough time. ☐
3 I spent all my pocket money. ☐
4 I couldn't get in. ☐
5 I got soaked in the rain. ☐
6 I didn't go to the party. ☐

a I didn't buy the CD.
b I caught a cold.
c I was tired the next day.
d I had a headache.
e I didn't finish my project.
f I lost my keys.

4 Look at Exercise 3 and write third conditional sentences.

1 *If I hadn't stayed up late, I wouldn't have been tired the next day.*

2 ....
3 ....
4 ....
5 ....
6 ....

could/should have done

We use *could(n't)* /*should(n't)* have + **past participle** to talk about events, actions and situations in the past. We usually imagine something which is in contrast to what really happened.

could(n't) have

We use *could(n't) have* + **past participle** to talk about:

• possibility
*Why did you take such a risk? You **could have been** killed!* (This was a possibility, but it didn't happen.)

- ability/opportunity
*Why didn't you ask me for help? I **could have explained** what to do.* (I had the ability to do this, but you didn't ask, so I didn't explain.) *You did your best. You **couldn't have done** any more.* (Even if you had tried harder/in a different way, it wouldn't have worked.)

should(n't) have

We use ***should(n't) have*** + **past participle** to talk about right and wrong. This includes:

- results
  *She **should have passed** the test – she tried really hard.* (This would have been the right result, but it didn't happen.)
- regrets/criticism (see below: *regrets and criticism*)
  *I **should have apologised** to him.* (This would have been the right thing to do, but I didn't do it.)
  *You **shouldn't have taken** the money.* (You did take the money, but it was the wrong thing to do.)

5 Complete the sentences with *could, couldn't, should* or *shouldn't* and the correct form of the verbs in brackets.

Why didn't you tell me you were having trouble with your project? I *could have told* (tell) you where to find information.

1 In the end it turned out OK, but things .... (go) terribly wrong.

2 Something's gone wrong with my chemistry experiment. It .... (start) bubbling like that.

3 The rocket .... (take off) at 4.20, but bad weather delayed the launch.

4 They didn't know what Tony was planning, and he was so determined that they .... (stop) him anyway.

5 He .... (be) a businessman like his father, but instead he chose to become an artist.

6 We booked a hotel room in advance, so there .... (be) any problem, but when we arrived, they said the hotel was full.

regrets and criticism

Regrets are the feelings we have when we realise that we have made a bad decision in the past – that is, we did something that was wrong, or didn't do the right thing.

Criticism is when we tell someone else that they did something which was wrong, or that they didn't do the right thing.

I wish and If only … !

We use *I wish* and *If only … !* to make statements about imaginary situations which are the opposite of what really happened; they show that we regret what really happened.

When we talk about the past, *I wish* and *If only* are followed by the past perfect.
I forgot about my mum's birthday. (what really happened)
*I **wish**/If only I **hadn't forgotten** about my mum's birthday!*

We can use *I wish* in the same way to criticise what someone else did or didn't do.
You lost my history notes. (what really happened)
*I **wish**/If only you **hadn't lost** my history notes!*

should(n't) have

We can also use ***should(n't) have*** + **past participle** to express our regrets or to criticise someone else's actions in the past.
I didn't check all the details. (what really happened)
*I **should have checked** all the details.*

6 Complete the second sentence so that it means the same as the first.

Why didn't you tell me that sooner?
If only *you'd told me that sooner!*

1 You borrowed my camera without asking.
You shouldn't ....

2 I watched a horror movie before going to bed.
I wish ....

3 Nicole didn't follow the instructions.
Nicole should ....

4 I left my mobile phone at home.
If only ....

5 Why weren't you more careful?
You should ....

6 I didn't do what you suggested.
I wish ....

8A Advertising

Vocabulary: shops and services

1 Match the sentences (1–8) with the shops and places in town (a–h).

| a supermarket | c travel agency | e hairdresser's | g library |
| b bookshop | d florist's | f bank | h chemist's |

1 Do you sell textbooks about marketing and advertising? ☐

2 Your prescription will be ready this afternoon, Mrs Jones. ☐

3 I'd like it really short at the back and long on top, please. ☐

4 We've got some special deals on package holidays to Mallorca. ☐

5 All the ingredients for baking are on the shelf next to the cakes. ☐

6 These books were due back last month. I'm afraid you'll have to pay a fine. ☐

7 Would you like to send a message with the roses, sir? ☐

8 I'd like to put €150 into my savings account, please. ☐

2 Circle the odd word out and write the name of the shop. Choose from the words in the box. There is one extra word.

| baker's butcher's chemist's greengrocer's |
| newsagent's post office shoe shop |

1 boots sandals trainers sweets

....

2 sausages pork rice chicken

....

3 stamps ham envelopes glue

....

4 a loaf rolls croissants make-up

....

5 socks potatoes lettuce mushrooms

....

6 toothpaste magazines newspapers greetings cards

....

3 Complete the sentences with the names of the places in Exercises 1 and 2.

1 If you're going to the .... later on, could you get me a copy of *The Daily News*?

2 Look at those fresh strawberries outside the .... Shall we buy some?

3 Go and get a trolley and I'll meet you inside the ...., next to the fruit section.

4 Tania fell over and cut her knee quite badly. Can you go to the .... and get some antiseptic cream?

5 I've got an appointment at the .... tomorrow morning. I'm going to have some blonde highlights put in.

6 I have to pick the tickets up from the .... before we leave for the airport.

7 When you go to the ...., can you ask him to chop the meat for me? I want to make a casserole.

Working with words: reporting verbs

4 Circle the correct option.

1 My sister *told / said* that she would help me with my homework.

2 The judges finally *announced / reported* that Johann was the winner.

3 The advertisement *asked / claimed* that the product could make people look younger.

4 The thief *denied / promised* that he had stolen my bike.

5 The newspaper *confirmed / thought* that the new supermarket would open on 3 November.

6 The bank manager *suggested / told* us that we couldn't borrow any more money.

5 Complete the sentences with the correct form of the verbs in the box.

| admit ask say suggest tell |

1 David .... that he was late because he had missed the train.

2 The teacher .... us that we had all passed the exam.

3 After three hours of questioning by the police, the gang finally .... that they had robbed the bank.

4 Joanne .... me if I would look after her cat while she was on holiday.

5 Tim .... that we buy Mrs Rice a watch as a leaving present.

Grammar: reported statements

6 Circle the correct option.

1 'Can I help you?'

The shop assistant asked if she *can / could* help us.

2 'This DVD won't work in my machine.'

The customer explained that the DVD *wouldn't / isn't going to* work in her machine.

3 'Andrew has bought a new computer.'

Isabel told me that Andrew *bought / had bought* a new computer.

4 'We're going to the shopping mall.'

Rachel said that they *went / were going* to the shopping mall.

5 'I'm working on a big advertising project.'

Penny told us that she *had been working / was working* on a big advertising project.

6 'The film starts at seven o'clock.'

Gary confirmed that the film *started / start* at seven o'clock.

7 Read the statements. What did the people actually say? Write their comments.

1 The designer claimed that each of his dresses was unique.

....

2 The pharmacist told me that they had run out of suncream.

....

3 The hairdresser asked me if I wanted my hair to be much shorter.

....

4 The prime minister stated that there was going to be an election in May.

....

5 The journalist reported that hundreds of people had been arriving at the refugee camp.

....

6 The man in the pet shop said that lizards made really good pets.

....

8 Read the blog. Then complete the sentences (1–7). Report what the people said. Change pronouns where necessary.

> Hi, I have to write about advertising at college. Can anyone tell me what makes a good TV advert?
> Danielle
>
> I think a good advert has to be funny.
> BloggerBoy
>
> A really catchy tune is essential.
> Jeremy
>
> Ford made a great advert in 2009, where they used car parts as musical instruments.
> Helena
>
> I know which advert Helena is talking about. It was really clever.
> Pixie
>
> Has anyone ever seen a good advert for cleaning products? They're usually really boring!
> Jon
>
> Cleaning is boring! But I'm sure that someone will make a cool advert for cleaning products one day!
> Alice

1 Danielle asked ....

2 BloggerBoy thought ....

3 Jeremy said ....

4 Helena said ....

5 Pixie said ....

6 Jon asked ....

7 Alice said ...., but that she ....

9 Write one word in each gap to complete the text.

What is a jingle and why is it important? We spoke to musician and jingle writer Richard Hall, who told [1]...................... that jingles [2]...................... basically catchy tunes written for TV advertisements. He said [3]...................... advertising agencies [4]...................... usually looking for tunes that [5]...................... sell a product. He explained that good jingles mentioned the name of the product several times. We [6]...................... him [7]...................... writing jingles [8]...................... difficult and he replied that it [9]...................... sometimes stressful because jingle writers [10]...................... to work under pressure.

8B Spending money

Reading

1 Read the article and choose the best two photographs (a, b or c) to illustrate the text.

Shoppers' Paradise

Dubai is one of the seven states which form the United Arab Emirates. In recent years, it has become a top tourist destination. Its exotic beaches, stylish hotels and first-class services attract people from all over the world. But these days, Dubai is probably best known for its shopping. It has more shopping malls than any other place in the world. It also has hundreds of traditional bazaars, called souqs, which sell everything from food and spices to silk and gold. But what does Dubai have to offer its younger visitors? We asked two British teenagers to tell us about their experiences.

'I went on holiday to Dubai with my family. At first, we spent a lot of time on the beach and going sightseeing. We saw some brilliant archaeological sites and even went on a camel ride, but it was just too hot! In the end, we decided to escape the heat and go to one of the big, air-conditioned malls. It was built in the shape of three pyramids and there were at least 300 stores inside, as well as coffee shops, restaurants and different entertainment centres. The shops were very stylish, but after a couple of hours, my younger brother said that he was fed up with looking round the shops, so I took him to an entertainment centre which had flying spaceships, a soft play area and arts and crafts. There was a great centre for teenagers too. It had a 3D animation theatre, indoor roller-blading and a live horror show. I went back there the next day with my dad and we had a brilliant time! I wish we had malls like that back in England!'
Kevin, Sheffield

'I loved the long, sandy beaches with their palm trees and sparkling, clear blue water. I could have stayed on the beach all day, sunbathing or snorkelling, but my parents wanted to look round the city. Although I didn't really want to go at first, I'm glad that I did! The city of Dubai is a really fascinating place. There is an amazing mix of traditional Arab buildings and huge, modern structures. There are massive squares with enormous fountains, beautiful mosques and glitzy hotels and office blocks – even the shopping malls are great to look at. We went to one mall, called Ibn Battuta Mall, which was built in six different styles: Andalusian, Iranian, Egyptian, Tunisian, Indian and Chinese. However, the best places for shopping, for me, were the souqs. They were colourful and lively, and the delicious smells of fruit and spices filled the air.'
Kayla, Dublin

2 Read the article again and answer the questions. Choose the correct answer (a, b or c).

1 What is modern Dubai most famous for?
  a its beaches and hotels
  b its shops and bazaars
  c its buildings and monuments

2 What did Kevin say about sightseeing in Dubai?
  a He had found it quite boring.
  b He had enjoyed visiting the sites.
  c He had not enjoyed the camel ride.

3 Why did Kevin's family decide to go to the shopping mall?
  a Because they wanted to go somewhere cooler.
  b Because they wanted to do some shopping.
  c Because Kevin's brother wanted to go to a children's play area.

4 Why did Kevin go back to the mall the next day?
  a To do some more shopping.
  b To help his dad choose some clothes.
  c To spend time in the entertainment centre.

5 How did Kayla feel when her parents suggested that they visit the city?
  a She would have preferred to stay on the beach.
  b She was annoyed with them.
  c She was happy to go with them.

6 What did Kayla enjoy most about the city?
  a the shopping malls
  b the architecture
  c the people

7 What was Kayla's opinion of the souqs?
  a She thought they were too crowded and noisy.
  b She thought they weren't as good as the malls.
  c She enjoyed the atmosphere.

Listening

3 🔘 *8.1* **Listen to John and Emma talking about money and shopping. Tick (✓) the items they mention.**

boots ☐   CDs ☐   clothes ☐   food ☐
football ☐   leather jacket ☐   notebooks ☐
pens ☐   phone credit ☐   shoes ☐

4 Circle the correct option.

1 John said he would probably *save / spend* most of his wages.

2 He said that he only earned *a little / a lot of* money.

3 John *fills shelves / serves customers* at the supermarket.

4 He *uses / doesn't use* his wages to buy clothes.

5 Emma thought she would be *good at / bad at* learning to budget.

6 Emma's parents give her money *whenever she asks for it / once a week*.

5 Complete the sentences with information from the dialogue. Write one or two words in each space.

1 Emma said that John should put his money in his ....

2 John usually spends his wages on .... and on going out.

3 John's mum puts money into his account once a ....

4 He couldn't afford new football boots because he had bought a ....

5 Emma said she usually .... with her mum when they went shopping together.

6 Emma is going to ask her mum if she would give her some money for .... every month.

Grammar: reported questions

6 Write direct questions.

1 Emma asked John what he was going to do with his wages.

....

2 She asked him if he bought his own clothes.

....

3 John asked Emma if she still had to ask her parents for money.

....

4 Emma asked her mum if she could have some money each month to buy clothes.

....

5 She also asked her when she had first learned to budget.

....

7 Report the questions.

1 Emma: 'How often do you work at the supermarket, John?'

....

2 Holly: 'Kate, have you ever used a credit card?'

....

3 Mike: 'Sam, where did you get your new trainers from?'

....

4 Kim: 'David, what are you going to buy with your birthday money?'

....

5 Teacher: 'Did you do your homework?'

....

Vocabulary: money

8 Complete the sentences with the words in the box.

| budget   coins   credit card   debit card |
| pocket money   savings   wages |

1 Young people in unskilled jobs often earn low ....

2 You can't get .... out of a cash machine – only notes.

3 When my grandfather retired, he spent his life's .... on a new house and a world cruise.

4 I've never learned to .... properly, so I'm always running out of money.

5 When I use my ...., the money comes straight out of my bank account.

6 If you use a ...., you have to pay at the end of the month.

7 I used to get quite a lot of .... when I was a child.

Useful expressions

1 Put the words in the correct order to form useful expressions.

1 I / you / help / can / ?

....

2 return / to / these / I'd / jeans / like

....

3 them / wrong / there / with / is / something / ?

....

4 the / you / receipt / have / got / ?

....

5 refunds / we / usually / afraid / don't / give / I'm

....

6 note / would / a / like / you / credit / ?

....

7 it / get / possible / be / to / would / money / back / my / ?

....

2 Complete the dialogue with the correct responses (a–f).

Assistant: Can I help you?

Customer: [1]...

Assistant: Is there something wrong with them?

Customer: [2]...

Assistant: Have you got the receipt?

Customer: [3]...

Assistant: OK. Would you like to exchange them for something else?

Customer: [4]...

Assistant: Really? Have you seen our new selection of DVDs?

Customer: I haven't got time to look right now.
[5]...

Assistant: Sorry. I'm afraid we don't usually give refunds. Would you like a credit note?

Customer: [6]...

Assistant: Six months, and you can use it at any of our branches.

a Would it be possible to get my money back, please?

b Yes, here it is.

c I'm not sure. How long is it valid for?

d No, thank you. I can't see anything I like.

e I'd like to return these earphones.

f Yes, they're faulty.

3 Complete the dialogues with the items in the pictures.

Assistant: Can I help you?

Customer: Yes. I'd like to return this bag of
[1]......................... .

Assistant: Is it past its sell-by-date?

Customer: No, it isn't. It should be all right for another three days, but the leaves have already gone brown and horrible!

Customer: I bought this [2]..................... yesterday but I'm not happy with it.

Assistant: Is there something wrong with it?

Customer: Yes, there is. The buttons have come off and there's a hole in the pocket.

DVD

Customer: The label on this box of [3]..................... says it's chocolate, but in fact it's coffee.

Assistant: OK. Would you like to go to the freezer section and exchange it for another one?

book

Customer: I bought this [4]..................... from you the other day, but I can't watch it. It says it's in English on the case, but it's in Dutch! Would it be possible to get my money back?

shirt

Assistant: I'm sorry, but we don't usually give refunds. Would you like a credit note?

Customer: I'd like to return this [5]..................... .

Assistant: Why? Is there something wrong with it?

Customer: Yes, there is. It's impossible to read! Half of the pages are missing.

ice cream

lettuce

4 Complete the dialogue with a word in each space.

Assistant: Can I help you?

Chloe: Yes, I'd like to ¹..................... this jacket.

Assistant: Why? Is there something ²..................... with it?

Chloe: No, not exactly. It was a birthday present, but I've already got one just like it.

Assistant: Oh, I see. Would you like to ³..................... it for something else?

Chloe: No, sorry. I can't see anything I like. Would ⁴..................... be possible to get my money ⁵.....................?

Assistant: I'm ⁶..................... we don't usually give ⁷..................... on clothes unless they are faulty. Would you like a credit ⁸.....................? It's valid for six months.

Chloe: Yes, OK.

Assistant: Great. Now, have you got a ⁹.....................?

Chloe: Yes, I think so. It should be in my wallet.

Pronunciation: syllable stress

5 🔘 *8.2* **Read the sentences and underline the stress in the words in italics. Then listen and check your answers.**

1 To *advertise* the new job, they put an *advertisement* in the job centre.

2 Most European countries are *democracies*, so they have a *democratic* system of government.

3 We wanted a *qualified* scientist, but his only *qualification* was a degree in history!

4 A: Are you interested in *politics*?
B: Yes, I'd like to be a *politician* one day.

5 I asked if they would *refund* my money, but they said they didn't give *refunds* on sale items.

6 The police want to reopen the *investigation*. They're going to *investigate* how the husband of the dead woman got all his money.

Writing: a formal letter

6 Read Tony's letter and answer the questions.

1 Who is he writing to?

2 What is he complaining about?

3 How many times did he have to complain?

4 What does he want the manager to do?

The Manager,
SuperShop, New Town

Dear Sir/Madam,
I am writing to complain about the quality of the fresh fruit and vegetables in your supermarket.
Two weeks ago, I bought a bag of lettuce leaves. The sell-by date said I still had four days left to eat them. ¹..................... this, when I got home, I realised they had already gone bad. So, I went straight back to the shop and complained to customer services. ²..................... of this bad experience, I returned to the supermarket a couple of days later, where I saw a sign advertising 'Fresh British Strawberries'. ³..................... this sign, I bought three boxes. However, when I got home, I discovered that all the strawberries underneath had gone soft and brown. What is more, ⁴..................... your claim that they were British strawberries, the label on the back of the box said 'Produce of Spain'. I went back to the shop and complained again.
⁵..................... of my complaint, I have not seen any improvement in the quality of the food. ⁶..................... this, I will not be shopping at your supermarket again unless the quality improves a lot. Please could you investigate the problem and reply to this letter as soon as possible?
Yours faithfully,
Tony Right

7 Read the letter again and complete the letter with *because of, despite* or *in spite*.

8 Think of a product or service you find in a supermarket, or use an idea from the box. Complete the notes about the problem. Then write your own letter of complaint.

> the shop assistants   the bakery
> the butcher's department   the car park facilities
> the check-out   the restaurant / café   the trolleys

What's wrong with the product/service?
....

What happened when I complained the first time?
....

What happened after that?
....

What I want the manager to do:
....

Reading

1 Read the note and choose the correct option (a, b or c).

> Hi Pete,
>
> I've had a look at the work you've done for our science project and I think you should have done more! How long did you spend on it? It can't have been more than a couple of hours. Susie and I have worked really hard and we've done twice as much as you! You also said you would do the artwork. I really hope you've done it! Please reply to this email ASAP.
>
> Claire

Why has Claire written to Pete?

a to make a suggestion

b to make a criticism

c to express regret

2 Read the note and choose the correct option (a, b orc).

> Hi Sarah,
>
> I bought a pair of jeans the other day. They were quite tight when I tried them on, but the shop assistant said they were supposed to be tight. Anyway, when I put them on at home, the zip broke! They must have been really badly made. Anyway, I'm going to take them back tomorrow and ask for a refund. Will you come with me, please?
>
> Jade

Why has Jade written to Sarah?

a to make a complaint

b to apologise for something

c to ask for her help

Language response

3 Read the statements (1–3) and choose the best option (a, b or c).

1 You phone a friend but she's not in. What do you say to her mother?

a Can I take a message?

b Can you ask her to call me back?

c Can you leave a message, please?

2 You are in a museum shop and have seen some souvenir mugs you like. What do you say to the assistant?

a Could I have a look at those mugs, please?

b What do you think of those mugs?

c Is it all right if I buy a mug?

3 Your friend asks to borrow your dictionary but you're using it. How do you respond?

a Because I'm using it at the moment.

b I'm sorry. I'm using it at the moment.

c Not at all.

Word list \ Unit 8

admit (v)	....	guarantee (n)	....
advert (n)	....	ham (n)	....
affect (v)	....	jar (n)	....
amount (n)	....	knee (n)	....
apart from (phr)	....	lizard (n)	....
appointment (n)	....	loaf (n)	....
arts and crafts (n pl)	....	mall (n)	....
attention (n)	....	mosque (n)	....
benefit (from) (v)	....	mug (n)	....
blackcurrant (n)	....	note (n)	....
branch (n)	....	pork (n)	....
brand (n)	....	prescription (n)	....
broadcast (v)	....	purchase (n)	....
button (n)	....	refugee (n)	....
cash (n)	....	refunds (n & v)	....
cash machine (n)	....	reply (to) (v)	....
casserole (n)	....	retire (v)	....
chart (n)	....	roller-blading (n)	....
coin (n)	....	savings (n pl)	....
come off (phr v)	....	savings account (n)	....
complain (v)	....	sell-by date	....
complaint (n)	....	snorkel (v)	....
confirm (v)	....	sparkling (adj)	....
customer (n)	....	stamp (n)	....
customer services (n pl)		sunburnt (adj)	....
deny (v)	....	underneath (adv)	....
due (back) (adj)	....	unique (adj)	....
emergency supply (n phr)	....	valid (adj)	....
enclose (v)	....	wages (n pl)	....
faulty (adj)	....	waste (n & v)	....
freezer (n)	....	yours faithfully (phr)	....
glitzy (adj)	....	zip (n)	....

reported statements

direct and reported speech

Direct speech gives the exact words someone said and uses quotation marks ('...') to show this.

Reported speech gives the meaning of what somebody said, but doesn't use all their exact words and doesn't use quotation marks. We use reported speech when we tell somebody else what another person said.

backshift

When we report what a person said, the time of speaking is not the same as the time of reporting. For example, what was the present at the time of speaking has usually already become the past at the time of reporting. For this reason, we often use backshift in reported speech, that is, the tense of a verb used in direct speech moves one step back into the past.

'I'm tired.' (direct speech: present simple)
*He said he **was** tired.* (reported speech: past simple)

*'We **have finished**.'* (direct speech: present perfect)
*They said they **had finished**.* (reported speech: past perfect)

other changes in reported speech

When we report what a person says, the place, listener(s), etc. at the time of speaking are often different to the place, listener(s), etc. at the time of reporting.

For example, imagine that on Monday, Gavin speaks to Cathy in the park: *'I'll see you here tomorrow,' Gavin said.*
On Friday, Cathy is at school, telling a friend about the conversation: what was 'tomorrow' when Gavin spoke is now several days ago, what was 'here' is now far away and so on. What Cathy reports is: *Gavin said he would see me there the next day.*

Words that change in reported speech include:

- *I, we → he/she, they*
- *me, us → him/her, them*
- *my, your, our → his/her, their*
- *this/these → that/those*
- *now → then/at that time*
- *last night/week/etc. → the night/week/etc. before/ the previous night/week/etc.*

- *this morning/afternoon/etc. → that morning/ afternoon/etc.*
- *next week/month/etc. → the next week/month/ etc./the following week/month/etc.*
- *yesterday → the day before/the previous day*
- *today → that day/the same day*
- *tomorrow → the next day/the following day*

1 Rewrite the sentences in direct speech.

A spokesman said the factory would close the following year.

'The factory will close next year,' a spokesman said.

1 He said that the company had been trying to solve the problem since the previous summer.

....

2 The manager told her that he hadn't been informed about her complaints.

....

3 She told him he would have to wait until the following week.

....

4 They told him that his company had to improve its image.

....

2 Report the statements.

'I know you were here yesterday, ' Avril told Sam.

Avril told Sam that she knew he had been there the previous day.

1 'I'm leaving for Paris tonight, but I'll be back soon,' he said.
He said that ....

2 'I've bought tickets for the concert this Friday,' Dan said.
Dan said that ....

3 'I don't think I'll be able to go to school tomorrow,' Angie said.
Angie said that ....

4 'I can't lend you my book now because I need it,' Joe told Fay.
Joe told Fay that ....

5 'We won't win today unless we play our best,' the captain said.
The captain said that ....

3 Rewrite the sentences in direct or reported speech.

'I'll stay here with the baby so you can go out,' he told Sue.

He told Sue that he'd stay there with the baby so Sue could go out.

1 She said that she'd never been there before in her life.

....

2 'I don't know why you keep losing your things!' she told them.

She told them ....

3 'I hate this kind of music!' he told us.

He told us ....

4 He told them that they would have to give him his money back.

....

reporting verbs

In direct speech, the exact words someone uses can show us if they are speaking politely, angrily, etc. In reported speech, where we don't use their exact words, we can use different **reporting verbs** to show this sort of information.
'Stop!' he shouted. → *He ordered me to stop.*
'Would you like to join us?' she told me. →
She invited me to join them.

Reporting verbs we use in this way include:
advise, ask, invite, order, remind, tell, warn. The normal pattern is **verb + object (+ *not*) + full infinitive**.
*She **told us** (**not**) **to leave**.*

There are other reporting verbs which don't follow the pattern above. These verbs include:

- *accuse sb of + -ing*
  They **accused him of stealing**.
- *admit + -ing*
  She **admitted lying** about the accident.
- *apologise for + -ing*
  I **apologised for being** late.
- *deny + -ing*
  He **denied taking** the money.
- *describe sth (to sb)*
  She **described the man** (**to the police officer**).
- *offer + full infinitive*
  I **offered to help** him.
- *refuse + full infinitive*
  She **refused to answer** my question.

4 Report the statements and questions. Use the correct form of the verbs in the box.

> advise   ask   invite   offer   suggest   tell

'Give me back my pencil, Judy,' Ronan said.
Ronan told Judy to give him back his pencil.

1 'How about watching TV?' Katy said.

....

2 'Shall I carry that bag for you, Wendy?' Mike asked.

....

3 'You should stay in bed,' the doctor said to her.

....

4 'Please turn your MP3 player down,' the man said to Marcus.

....

5 'Would you like to go out with me tomorrow, Fay?' Terry asked.

....

reported questions

A **reported question** begins with a phrase such as *She asked me ...*, and the rest of the reported question goes back to the word order of statements – that is, **subject + modal/auxiliary** (if there is one) + **verb**. Notice also that we use backshift, as in reported statements.
*What **do you do**?* (direct question)
*She asked me **what I did**.* (reported question)

If the direct question does not begin with a question word, we use the word *if* in the reported question. Again, the word order goes back to the word order of statements.
Do you use credit cards a lot? (direct question)
*She asked me **if I used** credit cards a lot.* (reported question)

5 Report the questions.

'Have you ever bought music online, Anna?' David asked.

David asked Anna if she'd ever bought music online.

1 'What are you doing for your birthday?' Ben asked Emma.

....

2 'Do you often go shopping?' Alan asked Fiona.

....

3 'How did you learn to cook?' Holly asked Dan.

....

4 'Are you interested in fashion?' she asked me.

....

Review Units 7 and 8

Grammar review: *wish* + past simple / past perfect

1 Circle the correct option.

1 My feet hurt! I wish I *bought / 'd bought* those trainers yesterday.

2 Marek's a vegetarian, but I didn't know. I wish I *didn't cook / hadn't cooked* chicken.

3 My printer isn't working. I wish this shop *sold / had sold* printer ink.

4 I didn't know it was your birthday. I wish I *brought / 'd brought* you some flowers.

5 I want to talk to Sally. I wish she *was / had been* here now.

6 I need to go shopping. I wish you *didn't take / hadn't taken* the car.

1 mark per item: ...... / 6 marks

Third conditional

2 Complete the sentences with the third conditional form of the verbs in brackets.

1 If I .... (save) more money, I .... (buy) a new computer.

2 If I .... (go) to bed earlier, I .... (not feel) so tired this morning.

3 Sam failed his exams again. .... (he / pass) his exams if he .... (study) harder?

4 If we .... (leave) earlier, we .... (not miss) the bus.

5 If I .... (not have) so much homework, I .... (come) shopping with you.

2 marks per item: ...... / 10 marks

3 Write third conditional sentences.

1 I didn't know it was so cold outside. I didn't wear a coat.

If ....
....

2 He forgot to take his phone. He didn't phone you.

If ....
....

3 We stopped to talk to our friends. We were late for the meeting.

If ....
....

4 She didn't put suncream on. She got sunburnt.

If ....
....

2 marks per item: ...... / 8 marks

Could/Should have done

4 Complete the sentences with *could/couldn't have* or *should/shouldn't have* and the correct form of the verbs in brackets.

1 Oh no! You .... (tell) her about the party – it was going to be a surprise.

2 My parents gave me some money for my laptop. It was expensive and I .... (afford) it without their help.

3 If she had run a bit faster, she .... (win) the race.

4 No, I'm sorry, I can't lend you my racket for the match. You .... (bring) your own.

5 They .... (get up) so early this morning. They'll be too tired to come out tonight.

2 marks per item: ...... / 10 marks

Reported speech

5 Report what the speaker said. Use the correct form of the reporting verbs in brackets.

1 My aunt: 'I'll phone you later.' (promise)

My aunt ....

2 Lucy: 'I didn't go to school because I was ill.' (explain)

Lucy ....

3 Paul: 'I've eaten all the cake.' (admit)

Paul ....

4 Teacher: 'The school is going to close at half past two.' (announce)

The teacher ....

5 Assistant: 'This cream is the best face cream on the market.' (claim)

The assistant ....

6 Weatherman: 'It's going to be hot and sunny.' (say)

The weatherman ....

7 Mum: 'Have you had anything to eat yet?' (ask)

Mum ....

8 Joe: 'I don't want to go out with you anymore, Sarah.' (tell)

Joe ....

2 marks per item: ...... / 16 marks

Vocabulary review: politics and science

6 Circle the correct option.

1 The prime minister has agreed to hold a(n) *election / protest* in May.

2 I don't agree with the government's *politics / policies* on education.

3 Emmeline Pankhurst helped British women win the *right / ability* to vote.

4 The ANC started a *campaign / party* of non-violent protests.

5 Nowadays, most countries in Europe are *democracies / governments*.

1 mark per item: ...... / 5 marks

7 Complete the sentences with words to do with science.

1 Albert Einstein's t...................... of relativity changed modern physics.

2 There have been many i...................... in technology in the last 20 years.

3 Despite ongoing r......................, scientists still haven't discovered a cure for the common cold.

4 The university has built a new science l...................... with the best modern equipment.

5 Scientists often have to do the same e................... many times before they get a result.

1 mark per item: ...... / 5 marks

Shops and services

8 Match the places (1–5) with the things (a–e).

1 baker's   **a** stamps
2 butcher's   **b** meat
3 chemist's   **c** magazines
4 newsagent's   **d** medicines
5 post office   **e** bread

1 mark per item: ...... / 5 marks

Money

9 Complete the dialogue.

A: How much [1]...................... .... do you get from your parents?

B: Not enough! But I earn quite good [2]...................... from my Saturday job at the supermarket.

A: That's good. Do you [3]...................... all the money you make, or do you manage to save some of it?

B: Well, at first, I put all my money in one bank [4]...................... and I took money out of the [5]...................... machine when I needed it, but I never managed to save anything. Now I put half of what I earn into a savings account. I don't use my debit [6]...................... to pay for things either. I always pay in cash.

1 mark per item: ...... / 6 marks

Prefixes and suffixes

10 Add prefixes to the verbs and write them in the correct form.

1 According to legend, the city of Atlantis .... under the sea. (appear)

2 I've forgotten my key, so I can't .... the door. (lock)

3 You should have .... the computer when the storm started. (connect)

4 The twins don't get on. They .... about everything! (agree)

5 Let's go to the beach. We can .... our bags later. (pack)

2 marks per item: ...... / 10 marks

11 Complete the sentences with the correct form of the words in the box.

| advertise   comfort   inform   investigate   qualification |

1 The rooms in this hotel are really ....

2 There are too many boring .... on TV these days.

3 The documentary was very .... I learnt a lot about black holes.

4 Karen is studying to be a doctor. She .... next year.

5 The police .... has been going on for three months, but with no success.

1 mark per item: ...... / 5 marks

Communicate

12 Write sentences and questions to complete the dialogue.

Alice: I / like / return / these trainers

[1]...

Assistant: be / something wrong / them / ?

[2]...

Alice: yes / be / too small / be / possible / money back / ?

[3]...

Assistant: afraid / not give / refunds

[4]...

Alice: Oh.

Assistant: you / like / exchange / something else / ?

[5]...

Alice: Not really.

Assistant: you like / credit note / ? / valid / six months

[6]...

Alice: Yes, OK.

Assistant: have / you / receipt / ?

[7]...

2 marks per item: ...... / 14 marks

Total: ...... / 100 marks

Welcome to Hollywood

How much do you know about Hollywood, the movie capital of the world and home to the stars? Read the text and complete the captions to the photos (a–f).

Hollywood's history

Hollywood is a neighbourhood of Los Angeles in California. It has a town centre and is surrounded by hills. On top of one of the hills stand the famous 15-metre-high letters that spell out the name *Hollywood*. The sign has been there since 1923 and was originally an advertisement for a new housing development called Hollywoodland.

The first film studio in Hollywood was called Nestor Studio and was built in 1911. For the next 70 years, Hollywood was the film and media capital not just of the US, but of the Western world. However, towards the end of the 20th century, things started to change. The film companies began moving away and building new studios outside of Hollywood. Now there is only one area of film set still left. This large space, called a backlot, belongs to Paramount Pictures and is used for filming outdoor scenes. Universal Studios have turned their studios into a visitor attraction and offer tours around sets from famous movies such as *Spartacus*, *Back to the Future* and Hitchcock's 1960 thriller, *Psycho*.

b

The Bates Motel, from Hitchcock's film ...., is a big attraction at Universal Studios theme park.

a

The famous Hollywood sign was originally a(n) .... for new housing.

Hollywood today

After the big studios moved away, the town of Hollywood lost its shine. Even though most of the other industries involved in film-making, such as editing, special effects, props and lighting, stayed in the town, the area started to become run down. In recent years, however, there has been a lot of redevelopment. Many old, abandoned buildings have been converted into expensive apartments. The old studios and historic theatres have become the venues for big concerts and award ceremonies. One example is the Hollywood Hotel, which is now the Kodak Theatre and is where the Oscars ceremony is held every year. Hollywood is also home to lots of scriptwriters, composers, camera operators, acting coaches, fitness coaches, producers, make-up artists, costume designers, photographers and acting agents, as well as some of the best doctors, dentists, vets and hairdressers in the world.

c

The Kodak Theatre, where the .... ceremonies are held, used to be a famous ....

Hollywood's Walk of Fame

Perhaps the most famous attraction in Hollywood, apart from its celebrities, is the Hollywood Walk of Fame. The Walk of Fame is just over two kilometres long and attracts about ten million visitors a year. More than two and a half thousand brass stars decorate the pavement along Hollywood Boulevard and each is dedicated to one of the stars of stage and screen. But it's not just actors and recording artists who have received a star. There are stars dedicated to make-up artists, costume designers and inventors, such as George Eastman, who invented roll film, and Thomas Edison, who invented the first film projector. Even Mickey Mouse, Donald Duck and Snow White have stars.

The names of more than .... famous people line the pavement on Hollywood's Walk of Fame.

Celebrity homes

If you want to meet a celebrity, Hollywood Boulevard is a good place to start. But you can also take a bus tour to the Hollywood Hills to see the multi-million dollar homes of famous celebrities such as Jennifer Lopez, Jim Carrey, Julia Roberts, Justin Timberlake, Christina Aguilera and John Travolta. Some of the most amazing houses include Meg Ryan's pink palace, Leonardo Di Caprio's beautiful white mansion and Jack Nicholson's huge house and gardens, which sit on the edge of a cliff. Most of these homes have spectacular views of the San Fernando Valley. However, although you can see the houses from the outside, you never get near enough to see any of the stars who live in them.

Hollywood dreams

Many young people come to Hollywood because they hope to find fame and fortune there. They dream of being 'discovered' by a great director and of becoming big stars. Unfortunately, their dreams rarely come true. If they are lucky, they get work as extras, but many of the people who chase the Hollywood dream find themselves working in bars and restaurants or, if they are very unlucky, end up homeless and living on the streets.

A .... person on Hollywood Boulevard

One of the beautiful, million-dollar houses in the .... area. Maybe someone famous lives here?

Answers:
a advertisement **b** *Psycho* **c** Oscar, hotel **d** 2,500 **e** Hollywood Hills **f** homeless

Sleep

1 Read the article about sleep and match the headings (a–f) with the sections (1–6).

    a Time for a siesta   **d** Human survival

    b Why do we dream?   **e** Why animals sleep

    c Dream time   **f** Why do we sleep?

Sleep

1 ....
We spend a third of our lives asleep, but researchers do not really understand why. Some sleep researchers believe that sleep keeps the brain functioning. Others say that sleep repairs damage from stress while we are awake, or that sleep helps you live longer. However, recent studies suggest other reasons why humans – and animals – need sleep.

2 ....
For many years, experts have thought that sleep was bad for survival because sleeping animals are more at risk from predators and can't perform essential activities such as eating, caring for family members, searching for food or looking out for danger. However, recent research suggests that animals can control their sleep behaviour. A team of experts studied a wide range of animals and found that the time an animal spends sleeping depends on its needs. These include migration needs, the need to care for its young and the need to avoid danger. For example, a small animal can't migrate to a warmer climate in winter, so it hibernates. As a result, it uses less energy and needs much less food. It also stays safe from predators by sleeping deep underground. On the other hand, migrating birds can fly for days without stopping or sleeping.

3 ....
Humans need to save energy too. Our brains weigh only two per cent of total body weight, but they use 20 per cent of our energy while we are awake. Sleep helps us to survive in lots of other ways too. For early humans, sleep helped to keep them safe because predators did not notice them when they were not moving about. Even now, we are much more likely to injure ourselves when we are tired, so having enough sleep is important for our safety. Like other mammals, humans can wake up quickly from sleep. The amazing thing about sleep is how the body and brain's metabolism can slow down while at the same time remaining responsive to their surroundings. A good example of this is that a parent will wake up if a baby makes even a small sound, but will sleep through a thunderstorm. When we are young, our high metabolic rate slows down a lot during sleep, but we sleep more deeply because there are people around to protect us.

b

Animals that don't migrate or hibernate can sleep peacefully. ....

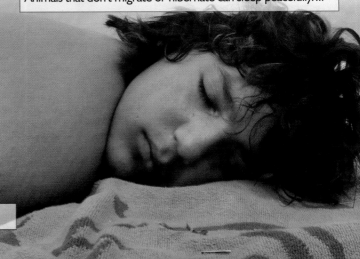

a   When humans sleep, their metabolism slows down, ...

2 Match the beginnings of the captions under the photos (a–d) with the endings (1–4) below.

1 ... because it helps their brains to develop. ☐

2 ... when they are not in danger or don't need to take care of their young. ☐

3 ... but they can still react to changes in the environment. ☐

4 ... because it helps the brain to process more information. ☐

c

It's good to have a nap during the day ...

4 ....

A good night's sleep improves our ability to learn much more than studying all night before an exam. A new study has shown that taking a nap also helps the brain process new information. It clears out space for the brain to take in new experiences. The study, by the American Association for the Advancement of Science in San Diego, asked 39 young adults to perform several learning tasks. One group then took a 90-minute nap, while the other group stayed awake. Afterwards, both groups performed the tasks again. The nappers performed much better than the non-nappers, the researchers found.

5 ....

After falling asleep, your muscles relax and you breathe more slowly. Then you go into a deep sleep and your eyes begin to move around quickly under your eyelids. During this rapid eye movement (REM) sleep, you dream. You may think you are performing physical actions, but your brain has frozen your muscles so that you actually lie still in bed. Thoughts and images flow into your mind, but they often seem strange and out of sequence.

6 ....

While you dream, your brain is sorting through all the experiences you have had while you were awake. Until now, it has stored them in temporary memory, but during REM sleep they are put into long-term memory. Babies need more REM sleep than adults. When a baby is born, many of the connections between neurons (nerve cells) haven't formed yet. As babies learn, each new experience or ability creates new connections, which are put into long-term memory during REM sleep.

d

Babies need more sleep than adults ...

3 Add one more sentence (1–4) to each caption.

1 We can wake up fast even in the middle of a dream.

2 It could even lead to better exam results.

3 Sleep is also important for animals' survival because it helps them to conserve energy.

4 They also sleep more deeply.

Indiana Jones

Are you an Indiana Jones fan? How much do you know about the ancient sites and artefacts in the films? Read the article and write the names of the artefacts and places in the captions (1–6). Then match the captions with the photos (a–f).

1 Some people believe these .... were made tens of thousands of years ago by an ancient civilisation. Others think that they were left by aliens who visited the Aztecs.

2 The eastern entrance to the .... temple is a 67-metre-high canyon called the ....

3 This is part of a wall painting which was discovered inside an Egyptian burial chamber in Egypt in 1886. It shows .... watching over a dead person.

4 The Aztec goddess of fertility, ... , was very complicated. She encouraged people to behave badly, but she also forgave them for their sins. The statue shows the goddess giving birth.

5 During the Shiva festival, Hindus bathe the sacred .... with milk and decorate it with flowers.

6 The .... of Ra appears in many examples of Egyptian art and was often found on jewellery. This amulet was discovered in the tomb of Tutankhamun.

Indiana Jones is a fictional character created by American film director George Lucas and played by Harrison Ford. Indiana Jones's real name is Dr Henry Walton Jones and he is a professor of archaeology. In order to rescue important artefacts from the 'baddies' who have stolen them, he becomes the brave adventurer Indiana Jones, or 'Indy' to his friends.

The mysterious objects that Indy tries to find and rescue are just as important as the characters in the films. Some of these artefacts are imaginary, but others, like the Ark of the Covenant or the Holy Grail, may actually exist, though no one knows for certain.

Raiders of the Lost Ark

This is the first of the four Indiana Jones adventures and is set in 1936. Indiana's mission in the film is to stop the bad guys from getting the Ark of the Covenant.

Tlazolteotl

In the opening scene of *Raiders of the Lost Ark*, Indiana Jones steals a golden statue of a goddess, Tlazolteotl, from an ancient cave in Central America. Tlazolteotl was the goddess of human fertility and motherhood in many South American cultures, including the Aztec culture. She often takes the form of a naked female.

The headpiece to the Staff of Ra

Before Indiana can get the Ark, he first has to find the headpiece to the Staff of Ra. When Indiana holds it up to the sun, it leads him to the room where the Ark of the Covenant is hidden. Although the Staff of Ra is an invented object, Ra is the name of the ancient Egyptian sun god and the creator of the world. The Eye of Ra is found

a

b

c

INDIANA JONES SITES AND ARTEFACTS – FACT OR FICTION?

on many Egyptian artefacts, especially wall paintings and jewellery.

Anubis

When Indy finally reaches the place in Tanis, Egypt, where the Ark of the Covenant is hidden, the room is guarded by an enormous statue of the Egyptian god of the dead, Anubis. Anubis has the head of a jackal and he watches over the dead. He weighs the dead person's heart in his hand to see if they were good while they were alive.

Indiana Jones and the Temple of Doom

The second Indiana Jones film is set in 1935, in India, where Indiana must find the Sankara stones and save a group of children from a bloodthirsty gang.

The Sankara stones

The Sankara stones are five short, stone columns based on the Shiva Lingam, which are found all over India in Hindu temples. The Shiva Lingam are cylindrical pieces of polished stone, like short columns, which symbolise Shiva, the Hindu god. Because they are an abstract symbol of God, the Shiva Lingam are considered to be very sacred and powerful objects.

The Cup of Kali

In the film, a gang of thuggees has taken the children of a village and is looking for the sacred Sankara stones. The leader of the gang, Mola Ram, has an ancient cup, called the Cup of Kali. His gang use the cup in secret ceremonies where they worship Kali, the Hindu goddess of death and destruction. In reality, 'thuggees' (where we get the modern English word *thug* from) did once exist in India. They were bands of highwaymen who robbed and murdered travellers.

Indiana Jones and the Last Crusade

The Canyon of the Crescent Moon

In this episode of the Indiana Jones adventures, he is looking for the Holy Grail. His search leads him to the Canyon of the Crescent Moon in the ancient city of Petra in Jordan. The real name of this canyon is the Siq and it leads directly to Al Khazneh, a spectacular but mysterious temple carved into the rose-coloured rock. According to the stories about the Holy Grail, it is one of the places where it may be hidden.

Indiana Jones and the Kingdom of the Crystal Skull

India Jones's last adventure takes place in 1957. Indy is enjoying a quiet life teaching when he suddenly finds himself in the middle of another race to rescue a lost artefact. This time he must rescue a crystal skull before agents of the Soviet Union get to it first. Crystal skulls do, in fact, exist, although they are very rare. There are only about twelve known examples in the world. Some people believe these skulls, which come from Mexico and Panama, are artefacts from the Aztec or the Mayan civilisations and that they have special powers.

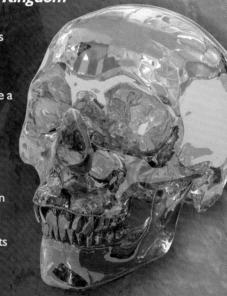

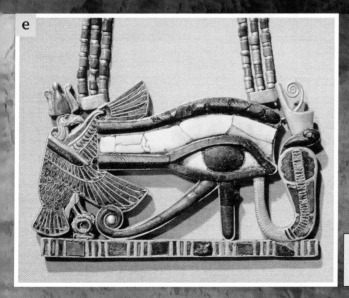

The Olympic Games

Read about the Olympic Games, past, present and future. Decide which Olympics the statements (1–10) refer to (there may be more than one). Tick (✓) the correct boxes.

QUIZ: True or false?

	Ancient Olympics	Modern Olympics	Future Olympics
1 You won't have to buy a ticket.	☐	☐	☐
2 There will be a spectacular opening ceremony.	☐	☐	☐
3 By the end of the games, you will have heard poetry, watched an animal die and seen new artists.	☐	☐	☐
4 Runners will bring a burning torch from Athens to the main stadium.	☐	☐	☐
5 The spectators will be cheering for their home teams.	☐	☐	☐
6 Winners will receive gold and silver medals.	☐	☐	☐
7 You will be standing up most of the time.	☐	☐	☐
8 The stadium will be environmentally friendly.	☐	☐	☐
9 Some athletes will be taking drugs to improve their performance.	☐	☐	☐
10 Athletes won't be wearing any clothes or shoes.	☐	☐	☐

The first games were held in Greece in the summer of 776 BC, almost three millennia ago. The ancient games were a fantastic festival dedicated to the god Zeus. It was a very religious event and was held in Olympia, where animal sacrifices and rituals used to take up as much time as the sports. There were also fire-eaters and palm readers as well as artistic events where new writers, painters and sculptors presented their work. Just as today, the games were held every four years. Rival city-states sent their fastest, strongest and most skilful men and boys to compete.

The names of the greatest Olympic athletes were known throughout Greece and their images appeared in sculpture and on pottery.

The site of the ancient Olympics at Olympia, Greece.

So, in what other ways were the ancient Olympics similar to the modern games of today? And how were they different?

Ceremonies and sporting events

First of all, the opening ceremony was just as spectacular as it is today. The naked athletes filed into the temple, where they stood before a terrifying statue of the god, Zeus, and promised to obey the rules of the game. A flame burned in each stadium, just as the Olympic torch burns today. However, the first torch relay didn't begin until 1936, at the Berlin Games.

Although there were lots of running races, the ancient games didn't have a decathlon or a marathon. However, there was a pentathlon, where the athletes had to run, wrestle, jump the long jump and throw the javelin and discus. The young male athletes were admired for their skill and beauty, and flute music was played during the long jump to celebrate this. The ancient Greeks also loved a good fight, especially a violent one. Wrestling and boxing were more brutal than today, with fewer rules and lots of injuries.

The ancient Olympics had no team sports. Athletes represented themselves first and their city-state second. There was no second place in the ancient games. Losers went home 'with their tail between their legs'.

Stadiums

In Olympia, there were three temples and a running track, but the stadium for the games was in the middle of nowhere. If you came from Athens, you had to walk 340 kilometres to get to the site. There were no toilets, no water and no seats. The word *stadium* comes from the Greek 'stadion', which means 'a place to stand'

and this is exactly what people did. However, entrance to all the events was free. Today's stadiums are huge, air-conditioned buildings with comfortable seats. Tomorrow's stadiums will be amazing designs using the latest green technology. A proposed design for the 2016 Rio de Janeiro games will use a spectacular waterfall and solar power to produce energy for the Olympic village.

Cheating

Throughout history, athletes have tried to cheat. Around the 4th century BC, the boxer Eupolus bribed his opponents to lose matches. When Emperor Nero took part in the chariot race, the judges let him win, even though he fell out of the chariot. You could buy special potions too, which were supposed to help improve your performance. These included a special medicine made of lizard skin. Today, 'doping' is a big problem in sport, with many athletes taking steroids and other drugs. In the future, the problem will be greater because of 'gene doping'. By the time of the next Olympics, some athletes will probably have started using drugs which alter their genes. Unlike other drugs, gene doping won't show up in existing tests.

Sportswear

Ancient Olympians competed naked and barefoot. Today's athletes wear technologically designed shoes and sportswear. In addition, new Olympic sports mean that scientists and designers will continue to develop new sports gear. The 2008 Olympics introduced us to 'supersuits' for swimmers and advanced shoes for marathon runners. It will be interesting to see what designers will invent for the next Olympics.

A referee watches Greek wrestlers during a fight at the Olympic Games.

Technologically designed sportswear, needed for the new Olympic sport of open-water swimming.

Answers:
1 Ancient   2 all three
3 Ancient   4 Modern and Future   5 Modern and Future   6 Modern and Future
7 Ancient   8 Future
9 all three   10 Ancient

Reading Explorer

Marco Polo

1 **Who was Marco Polo? Read the text and choose the best answer (a, b or c).**

   a An Italian merchant in the 12th century who travelled to India and Iran

   b An Italian explorer who lived with the Chinese royal family for many years

   c An Italian merchant and explorer in the 13th century who travelled widely in Asia.

2 **Read about Marco Polo's journey and look at his route on the map. Write the cities and islands in the correct places on the map.**

Acre Constantinople Hormuz Jerusalem Tabriz Shangdu Sumatra Venice

Marco Polo was a young merchant in Venice back in the 13th Century. In 1271, he left Italy with his father, Niccolò, and his uncle, Maffeo, and travelled across more than 7,500 miles to the old Mongolian city of Shangdu. Three years later, Marco finally entered the shining marble palace of the Kublai Khan about 200 miles north-west of Beijing. Very few Europeans had journeyed so deep into Asia before or had spent so long travelling.

Marco Polo wrote about his experiences in his book *Description of the World*, but when the Venetians read about Marco's wonderful adventures, he was not taken seriously. The idea that the world's largest and richest cities were not found in Europe was a huge shock to them. Marco also wrote about things which Europeans had never seen, but the animals and places he described were too strange. People did not believe him. Even today, there are still people who think he invented the whole story.

So how much of Marco Polo's book is true? Some people argue that Marco went no further than Constantinople or the Black Sea, and that his more fantastic stories were stolen from Arabs and Persians he met there. However, academics who have studied his work believe that most of it is true, but say that Marco's work was changed by the monks and scribes (writers) who copied and translated it. About 150 different versions of Marco Polo's text are known to exist. The version which is probably closest to Marco's original belongs to the Bibliothèque Nationale in Paris.

Marco left Venice, aged 17, with his father and uncle. They sailed first to Constantinople (now Istanbul), in Turkey, where Marco was impressed by the fantastic bazaars and wrote about the fine carpets and silk. From there, the Polos sailed to Acre, then travelled to Jerusalem and then onto Tabriz, in the north-west corner of Iran. The city used to be popular with Italian merchants who wanted to buy goods from strange lands, especially the rubies and sapphires from India and Sri Lanka. Today, it is a modern city of concrete buildings, except for the enormous bazaar, with its massive brick walls and elegant arches.

Europeans and Arab sheikhs still visit the bazaar in Tabriz to buy carpets and jewellery.

Marco Polo

Mongolia

•7

Turkey

•2

•5

China

•1

•3

Israel

•4

•6

India

Marco Polo's journey across Europe and Asia covered more than 24,000 miles.

The Kublai Khan had a passport made for Marco. It was similar to this one, but instead of being made of iron and silver, it was made of gold.

•8

After travelling across Persia, the Polos reached the port of Hormuz. They decided not to travel by sea to India and China because they did not trust the Persian traders' ships. 'Their ships are very bad and many of them are lost,' wrote Marco. Instead, they travelled along the Silk Road, over the Central Asian mountain range. Marco described the mountains as 'the highest place in the world'. He also recorded seeing huge, wild sheep with enormous horns, which became known as Marco Polo sheep.

The three men then had to cross the Gobi desert before reaching their destination: the palace of the Kublai Khan. Niccolò and Maffeo had been there nine years before. The Polos stayed at the palace and Marco became the Kublai's advisor and ambassador. He travelled the four corners of the Mongolian Empire and recorded all the fascinating things he saw: the local customs and events, clothes, religions and wildlife. In southern China, he met people whose sharpened teeth were covered in gold and whose bodies were decorated with tattoos.

After 17 years, the Kublai Khan finally allowed the Polos to leave. They travelled to Persia with a Mongol princess. Carrying gold and rubies, they sailed from the Chinese coast via Sumatra and Sri Lanka. After delivering the princess to her future husband, they eventually reached Venice 24 years after they had left.

In Marco Polo's day, the mountains of central Asia were very difficult to cross.

3 Complete Marco Polo's notes with information from the article.

Constantinople
Fine [1]...................... and [2]...................... cloth are sold here.
Tabriz
The huge [3]...................... here is made of [4]...................... .
I met another Italian merchant who said he had come here to buy [5]...................... and [6]...................... from India.
Central Asia
These must be the highest [7]...................... in the world!
Today I saw some enormous [8]...................... sheep. Their [9]...................... were as long as my leg!
China
The people in southern China look very different. Their bodies are covered in [10]...................... and their [11]...................... have been made very sharp.

Monster myths

1 **Read the text and match the names of the monsters (1–4) with the continents where they are found (a–d).**

1 Abominable Snowman   **a** North America
2 Bigfoot   **b** Europe
3 Loch Ness Monster   **c** Central Africa
4 Mokele-Mbembe   **d** Asia

Monsters of legend

There are many legendary monsters around the world. For centuries, people have told stories of strange mountain beasts and of mysterious creatures living in lakes. People everywhere, it seems, love a good monster mystery.

Bigfoot

One autumn day in 1967, deep in the mountains of northern California, two men saw a huge, hairy beast sitting by a stream. The creature then walked off into the forest. Luckily, the men managed to film the beast on their video camera. They also made plaster casts of the creature's enormous footprints, which they found in the mud. In California, this monster is known as Bigfoot. In Canada it's called Sasquatch, which comes from an Indian word that means 'wild people'. But does Bigfoot really exist? Some scientists say that the film and footprints are fakes. And if the story of Bigfoot was true, surely someone would have found a body or a skeleton of one by now. They might even have caught a live one!

The Yeti

For centuries, people in Tibet and Nepal have been telling tales about a huge, hairy, smelly, ape-like creature that lives on the slopes of the Himalaya mountains. The beast has many names, including the Abominable Snowman and the Yeti, which means 'big eater'. During the 20th century, there was a lot of interest in the Yeti. British and American explorers and mountaineers reported seeing a large, human-like creature wearing no clothes. They photographed strange, enormous footprints in the snow and even brought back hair samples.

In recent years, however, DNA tests have shown that the hair was from different wild animals that live in mountains. Scientists also suggest that the Yeti might actually be a threatened species of Himalayan Brown Bear, which can walk upright.

These footprints may have been made by a Himalyan bear. Or do they belong to the Yeti?

The sign on this tree might persuade more people to stop and visit 'Bigfoot country'.

The Loch Ness Monster

The Loch Ness Monster is probably the most famous lake monster in the world. People have reported seeing the marine reptile for more than 1,300 years. They say it has a long neck and spikes on its back, like a dragon. In 1934, a man claimed that he had taken a photo of Nessie. But in 1991 he told reporters that it was a fake. The photo really shows a model which he had stuck onto a toy submarine.

Over the years, researchers have searched the lake using modern equipment such as underwater cameras and ultra-sonic sensors. Although they have never found Nessie, they have learned a lot about the lake. They believe that there would have to be many more fish in the water to feed a large predator. Also, the lake would be too cold for any large reptile to survive. There is a theory that the Loch Ness Monster could actually be a huge fish, called a sturgeon. The sturgeon has a long nose and a spiky back and can grow to 20 feet long. It lives in the North Sea, but one may have swum into the lake and been seen before swimming away again.

Mokele-Mbembe

For years, people have reported seeing a strange beast, known as Mokele-Mbembe, in the swampy lakes and jungles of Central Africa. If it exists, this creature could be the last living dinosaur on Earth. However, descriptions vary. It may look like a brontosaurus, but in other parts of the Congo, native pygmies say it looks similar to a huge rhinoceros. There have been many expeditions into the dangerous lakes and swamps to find Mokele-Mbembe, but so far there is no proof that the beast exists at all.

2 Test your knowledge. Write the names of the monsters.

1 These monsters are covered in hair. ....

2 This beast was captured on film. ....

3 This animal could be a dinosaur. ....

4 These beasts are able to walk like humans. ....

5 Advanced technology has been used in the
   search for this beast. ....

6 If it existed, this beast would die of hunger. ....

7 People have taken photographs of its footprints. ....

8 This creature might actually live somewhere else. ....

Could Nessie really be just a large fish?

Answers:
1 1 d 2 a 3 b 4 c

2 1 Bigfoot and the Yeti
2 Bigfoot   3 Mokele-Mbembe
4 Bigfoot and the Yeti
5 The Loch Ness Monster
6 The Loch Ness Monster
7 the Yeti   8 The Loch Ness Monster

Could this be a picture of the last living dinosaur on Earth?

Darwin's voyage of discovery

1 Read about Darwin's voyage and write the discoveries (a–d) in the boxes (1–4) on the map.

a lesser rhea

b extinct camel

c rhea Americana

d Pleistocene giants

a three-toed sloth

BOLIVIA

PARAGUAY

URUGUAY

ARGENTINA

Pampas Region

1

2

Monte Hermoso

CHILE

Punta Alta

3

Northern Patagonia

4

a vicuña

lesser rhea in Patagonia

In 1831, a 22-year-old naturalist called Charles Darwin joined a British expedition to survey the coast of South America. The team was travelling by ship, the HMS Beagle, and during the five years of expedition, Charles Darwin wrote a diary about his experiences and his thoughts on science. This diary later became a famous travel book called *The Voyage of the Beagle.* This voyage, and all that Darwin thought and wrote about on board the Beagle, turned out to be the beginning of a revolution in natural science.

The early discoveries

In September 1832, when the Beagle expedition was surveying in Argentina, Darwin made his first discovery. At a place called Punta Alta, he found the fossils of nine huge animals, most of which were unknown to science. These animals were extinct Pleistocene giants – a set of species of large animals, mammals, birds and reptiles that lived on Earth during the Pleistocene period, 12,000 years ago. What Darwin found included an animal like a sloth, but big as an elephant, and skeletons that resembled those of a horse and an armadillo.

A month later, and 30 miles up the Argentinian coast in a place called Monte Hermoso, Darwin found the fossil of an extinct camel. Darwin began to ask himself if this could be the ancestor of the South American vicuña and llama. He sent the fossils he had collected to his old professor at the University of Cambridge. In the Pampas region, Darwin also ate a rhea Americana, a large, heavy bird, similar to an ostrich.

Several months later, the expedition reached Patagonia where Darwin noticed people eating a bird called the lesser rhea, which was very like the rhea Americana, but much smaller. Although they were similar, the two species were also different in several ways. Was this because they inhabited very different areas – the Pampas, a fertile grassland, and northern Patagonia, which is dry and stony?

Darwin's theories

When he set out on the voyage, Darwin believed, like all Christians at the time, that God had created each species separately and had put them in different parts of the world; kangaroos in Australia, giraffes and zebras in Africa, rheas and sloths in South America and so on. But after his observations in South America – and later when recording the many similar but slightly different species of giant tortoise found on the Galapagos Islands – Darwin began to feel that there must be another explanation. The fossils he had found were very similar to living species, which suggested that they must be related. The similarity of the rheas living in different areas suggested that they too had descended from an earlier species of rhea.

But can one species really change into another? Darwin spent eighteen months thinking about this question and eventually concluded that animals have to adapt to their environment in order to survive. The species that survives passes these physical changes on to the next generation. Darwin called this process 'natural selection' and continued to develop his ideas for twenty years. In 1859, he published his book *On the Origin of Species by Means of Natural Selection*. It was a great success. Three years later, Darwin published his second book, *The Descent of Man*, which argued that human intelligence could have evolved by natural selection in ape-like ancestors. The public were shocked and horrified.

Was Darwin right?

Nowadays, of course, the theory of evolution is very widely accepted and no longer considered shocking. Moreover, genetic research has begun to prove Darwin's theories to be correct. In 2003, geneticists found that the human genome was very similar to the chimpanzee genome – proof that all hominids are descended from a common ancestor. If Darwin had been around in 2004, the discovery of the Tiktaalik* would have made his dreams come true. This 375-million-year-old fossil was clearly a fish, with scales and fins, but it also had a flat, amphibian head and a neck. The bones inside its fins looked like arm and wrist bones. This was the missing link which showed how animals had evolved from sea to land.

* The Tiktaalik provides important clues to the story of evolution.

2 **Find the words in the text and complete the crossword.**

Across

6 This happens when animals develop new physical characteristics in order to survive.
7 These cover the body of a fish.

Down

1 A different species of this animal is found on each of the Galapagos Islands.
2 Orang-utans, gorillas, chimpanzees and humans belong to this super-family of apes.
3 An animal that can live on land and in water.
4 A person that was related to you but that died long ago.
5 All the hereditary information about an organism, including DNA, is encoded in this.

Answers:
1 1d 2c 3b 4a
2 **Across:** 6 natural selection 7 scales
Down: 1 giant tortoise 2 hominid 3 amphibian 4 ancestor 5 genome

In this photo, a young girl from Laos is wearing her family's wealth on a silver coin vest.

The first stamped coins showed a turtle from the Aegean Sea.

Money

1 **What was the earliest unit of currency? Read the text and choose the best answer (a, b or c).**

a the electrum   **b** the shekel   **c** the cowrie shell

2 **Complete the text with the words in the box.**

exchange   gold   jewellery   metals   silver   fruit

Early forms of currency

Many people believe that ancient civilisations exchanged food, such as wheat and [1] .... for other food and services. However, this would not have been possible because different food was harvested at different times of the year. If a fruit farmer wanted to exchange his produce for wheat, his fruit would have gone bad before he had the chance to trade. As a result, people traded using items that did not go bad and that were highly valued. These early forms of currency included gold, silver, copper, wine and salt. In Africa, cowrie shells and ivory [2] .... were highly valued. There is evidence that the Early Egyptians used gold bars as far back as 4,000 BC.

Cowrie shells, like these from Myanmar, are still a form of currency in *tribal* cultures.

Shekels were the first ever unit of currency and were introduced by the Babylonians in Ancient Egypt. These coins were made from [3] .... , bronze or copper. A shekel was both a unit of currency and a weight. One shekel was equivalent to a specific weight of barley. People could [4] .... barley for shekels and then trade their shekels for other goods from neighbouring city states.

The first stamped coins were made in Ancient Greece around 700 BC. They were made of a mixture of gold and silver and other [5] .... , called electrum or white gold. The coins, which were produced by the government, were stamped with an image of a turtle, to prove that they were authentic. Although gold and silver coins were originally of equal value, [6] .... eventually became more valuable in Europe than any other metal.